The Art & Character of

# NUTCRACKERS

*By Arlene Wagner*

THE LEAVENWORTH NUTCRACKER MUSEUM
A NATIONAL HERITAGE FOUNDATION

*Decorative Metal Lever Nutcracker*
20th Century, United States
Sterling (handles), Stainless Steel (cracking mechanism);
6.5" (16.5 cm)

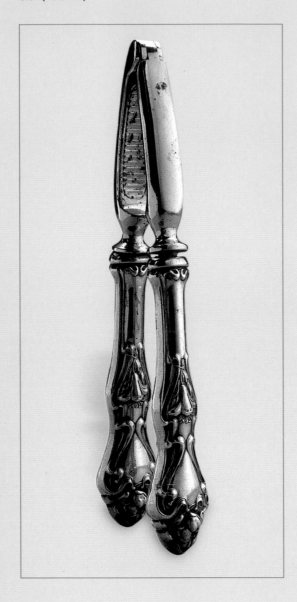

A SINCERE THANK YOU to the team at Arscentia for helping to make this book a reality—to Michael McIvor for the wonderful book design, Dan Hansen for color management, Ric Peterson for photography, and the numerous other Arscentia staff for their hard work and dedication to this project.

Collectors Press books are available at special discounts for bulk purchases, premiums, and promotions. Special editions, including personalized inserts or covers, and corporate logos, can be printed in quantity for special purposes.

For a free Collectors Press catalog or for further information, write to:

**COLLECTORS PRESS, INC.**

P.O. Box 230986
Portland, OR 97281
Toll free: 1.800.423.1848 or visit our website at: www.collectorspress.com

Design: ARSCENTIA, SEATTLE

Copy: Arlene Wagner, Lori Kothe
Editor: Jan Lorey Hood
Proofreader: Julie Steigerwaldt

Printed in Singapore

First American Edition

9 8 7 6 5 4 3 2 1

Library of Congress Cataloging–in–Publication Data

Wagner, Arlene, 1924-

The Art & Character of Nutcrackers
The Leavenworth Nutcracker Museum: A National Heritage Foundation

by Arlene Wagner—1st American ed.
         p.     cm.
Includes bibliographical references.
ISBN 1-933112-08-5 (hardcover: alk. paper)
1. Nutcrackers (Implements)—Collectors and collecting. I. Title: The Art & Character of Nutcrackers. II. The Leavenworth Nutcracker Museum. III. Title.

NK8551.3.W34 2005
683'.82—dc22
                    2004027561

# Table of Contents

*Dutch Character*
1850, Germany (Southern Region)
Conifer; 14.5" (37 cm)

passionate

# The Leavenworth Nutcracker Museum Story

We are often asked how The Leavenworth Nutcracker Museum came to be, and here is the story. In the 1970s and 1980s, I was artistic director for Ballet Les Jeunes, a small ballet company in Renton, Washington, that produced *The Nutcracker* ballet each year. Like Clara in the story, I became entranced with the toothy, wooden nutcracker.

My husband, who at the time was a real estate broker, also became fascinated with the toy soldier nutcrackers, and together we started collecting them. Then, at a large antique show, we discovered beautifully carved figural nutcrackers from Switzerland, intricate brass ones from England, and silver-plated ones from the United States. Of course, we were familiar with the kitchen tool in the drawer at home, but we had no idea that such wondrous specimens existed. *We were hooked!*

Throughout the following years, we hunted for nutcrackers across Europe and the United States. We searched antique shops and attended antique shows. We frequently visited Germany's mountainous Erzgebirge region and became acquainted with many of the artisans. We met with other collectors who shared our passion. We read every bit of information we could find on the endless variety of nutcrackers. As the number of nutcrackers in our collection grew into the thousands, it attracted worldwide attention. Antique dealers from the United States, Germany, England, France, Italy, and the Netherlands would contact us with a new "find." In fact, without these dealers we could not have gathered such an impressive collection—to them we are grateful.

Now that we are eighty years old and have amassed a 5,000-piece collection, we are eager to share it—with this generation and many to come. That is why the entire collection has been donated to The Leavenworth Nutcracker Museum, a National Heritage Foundation.

While the museum serves as the stage to display these grand "characters," this book serves as our photo album, a storybook to peruse and enjoy. All photos on these pages depict nutcrackers that belong to The Leavenworth Nutcracker Museum, or to Claudia Davis (a museum board member), whose collection someday will join the museum. Many of the specimens were formerly in the well-known European collections of Ortrud and Hans Jürgen Gillissen of Germany and David Levi of England.

Although—when possible—we have provided the country of origin and date of the nutcrackers, this book is not intended to qualify as a scientific publication. In fact, we know that in many instances there will be disagreement. Some of our nutcrackers have been given three or four different origins or dates by those considered to be experts. This in itself indicates the difficulty of being absolutely correct.

We are especially grateful to Rik Gijsen of the Netherlands for his help in organizing this book and for sharing his vast knowledge with us. We also want to thank Uwe Löschner of the Erstes Nussknacker Museum Europas, Germany, and Dr. Barbara Sharon, a fellow Washingtonian, for their expertise in Erzgebirge folk art; Robert Mills of England for his generous help and encouragement; Mary Barthel of Germany for identification of woods; and Susan Otto and members of the Nutcracker Collectors Club for providing pertinent information. To Judith Rittenhouse, who was brave enough to write the first history of nutcrackers, we give a special "thank you," for we will be eternally grateful for her endeavors.

—Arlene Wagner, *The Nutcracker Lady*

*Soldier*
1880, Germany (Erzgebirge)
Spruce; 10.75" (27.5 cm)
*(crafted by Wilhelm Füchtner, "Father of the Nutcracker")*

## Introduction:
# From Soup to Nuts

Over the years, man has created ingenious ways to open the nutshell. No other collectible or tool has shown such a diversity of materials and design as the nutcracker. The first nutcrackers were undoubtedly hammers or simple utilitarian designs, probably two pieces of wood hinged at one end with leather straps. Today, many specimens exist that can truly be called works of art.

*Lever Carved from Single Piece*
Late 16th/Early 17th Century, England
Ash; 6.25" (16 cm)

## Nutcrackers Throughout the Ages

Nutcrackers have a long and fascinating history that embodies both creativity and culture. A bronze nutcracker in the form of two hands was discovered in 1930 in a grave near Tarente, Italy. It has been dated to the third or fourth century B.C. Bracelets of gold adorn the wrists, which serve as handles for the nutcracker.

Iron nutcrackers from the 13th century are recorded in Henry René D'Allemagne's book, *Decorative Antique Ironwork*. Henry VIII is said to have presented a carved-wooden nutcracker to Anne Boleyn, one of his wives. During Shakespeare's time, nuts were eaten at the theater much as people eat popcorn today. This was evidenced by the large number of hazelnut shells found when the Rose Theatre was excavated. In the Victorian period, fruit and nuts were served at the end of the meal, from which came the phrase, "from soup to nuts."

## Evolution of the Nutcracker

Many factors—from purely practical to purely stylistic and expressive—have contributed to the evolution of the nutcracker's form, functionality, and character. These factors include advances in production techniques, the availability of materials, styles of the time, consumer demand, and even changes in the nuts themselves.

For example, the nut receptacle of early nutcrackers was very small to accommodate the uncultivated hazelnut (or cobnut). As horticulture improved the size of the nut, the size of the nutcracker also changed. Larger receptacles were made for walnuts, and special nutcrackers were made for pecans that cracked the nut from the ends to assure a whole kernel.

Aesthetically, nutcrackers have often reflected the cultural values and innovations of their place and date of origin. From the Romanesque, Gothic, Renaissance, and Baroque periods to the incredibly individual and eclectic styles of the 19th and 20th centuries, nutcracker designs have evolved to include everything from ornate sterling nut openers worthy of inclusion in the finest Victorian silver services to the wooden toy soldiers associated with Christmas.

Turned Wooden Toy Soldiers:
Soldier, Prince, and King
Late 20th Century, Germany (Erzgebirge)
Linden; [from left to right] 11.75" (30 cm);
15.5" (39.5 cm); 9" (23 cm)
(from the Seiffener Nussknackerhaus)

Indirect pressure is best explained by looking at a pair of pliers. Here the nut is cracked on the other side of the fulcrum, away from the hand. The wooden toy nutcracker, the type so popular at Christmas, is a good example of this action.

There are metal nutcrackers that employ both direct and indirect methods. Smaller nuts are cracked by the shorter jaws, while larger nuts are cracked between the handles. Most of the carved wooden heads in human and animal forms have a recessed place between the handles to crack larger nuts that do not fit in the mouth, and to protect the beautifully carved facial features from damage.

### Screw

The screw mechanism gives greater control over the pressure being applied to crack the nut. It is easier to get a whole kernel with the screw type than with the crushing blow of the hammer or the forceful compression of the lever types. Metal screw nutcrackers are known to have existed in the 16th century, and wooden screw nutcrackers first appeared in England in the 17th century.

## Nut-Cracking Methods

The cracking of nuts can be accomplished in several ways, but most nutcrackers use the percussion, lever (direct and indirect pressure), or screw method.

### Percussion

With the percussion method, the nutshell is broken by striking it with an object such as a rock, hammer, or plunger device. Sometimes special hammers were made specifically for cracking nuts. In 1850 a "knee warmer" was developed in America. This was a curved cast iron base which fit over the upper leg. A raised, curved pedestal in the middle of the base held the nut while it was struck with a hammer.

### Lever

Made in both wood and metal, lever nutcrackers use direct or indirect pressure to crack the nutshell. Direct and indirect lever nutcrackers are differentiated by which side of the fulcrum (the point where the lever pivots) the nut is cracked. Direct pressure is used when the nut is cracked between the fulcrum and the hand. When one lever rotates 360 degrees to accommodate a different size of nut, this method is called "reversible" or "flip-over."

*Percussion Knee Warmer*
1850, United States
Iron; 3" (7.5 cm)

*Ring Screw*
1890, Scandinavia
Wood; 3.75" (9.5 cm)

*Kangaroo Lever*
1930, England
Iron; 5.5" (14 cm)

*Communal Nutting Stone*
Middle Archaic Period (est. 5,000–8,000 years old),
United States (Arkansas)
Stone; [w] 15.5" (39 cm) x [h] 5" (12.5 cm)
*(A pair of hammer stones are displayed on the nutting stone.)*

## Common Nutcracker Materials:
# Stone

Nuts have been a significant part of the food supply since the beginning of time. Excavations of early civilizations have revealed nutshells, probably broken by two stones when too hard for the teeth to crack.

Artifacts | On the site of Gesher Benot Ya'aqov, close to the Dead Sea in Israel, archaeologists discovered seven varieties of nuts that they reported to be 780,000 years old. Along with these nuts, some fifty pitted stones were found with at least one depression that appears to have been formed by repeated usage in the cracking

*Dated to the Late Archaic Period (est. 3,000–5,000 years ago), this 5.5" (14 cm) nutting stone was found in Sweden.*

of nuts. The nuts and the stone tools found with them are the first evidence that various types of nuts formed a major part of prehistoric man's diet, and that these early peoples had developed an assortment of tools to crack open the nuts.

Similar stone tools found in many parts of the United States have been dated back to the Archaic Period, 4,000–8,000 years ago. The peoples of this time were nomadic and would camp near the nut trees when it was time for the nuts to fall. Kernels were eaten whole, or ground with mortar and pestle to make flour or nut butters. Nuts used were beechnuts, chestnuts, and hickory nuts. Many times the nutmeats were cooked, and when the broth cooled, the congealed fat would be taken off and saved for later use. The shells were used to fuel the nomads' fires. Since the nuts stayed fresh for a long period of time in their shells, they were carried with the people when they moved their camp.

*Early Native Americans would place a nut in the depression of the "nutting stone" and then hit it with another stone called the "hammer stone."*

*Various Nutting Stones*
Middle Archaic Period (est. 5,000–8,000 years old),
United States (Louisiana/Alabama/Arkansas/Ohio)
Stone; [largest] 6.5" (16 cm)

# Wood

Whether turned on a lathe or carved by hand, many different kinds of wood have been used to make nutcrackers. Usually the makers used the wood from trees that grew in their locality. Master carvers preferred boxwood because of its uniform light warm color and its fine grain that enabled them to do delicate carvings.

Conifer trees, also known as "needle" trees, include pine, cedar, spruce, and fir. Deciduous, broadleaf trees include linden, birch, beech, ash, oak, maple, and wood from nut and fruit trees. Today linden and beech are the preferred woods for making nutcrackers; however, birch, spruce, and pine are also used. Harder woods such as maple are used for turning very small items.

*Wood must be dried to approximately eight percent moisture content before it can be carved or turned. This usually requires drying the wood outside for several years, then inside until the desired moisture content is reached.*

*Man in Top Hat*
1900, France
Boxwood; [height] 3.5" (9 cm)

*Table Screws*
[left] 19th Century, England; [right] Middle 20th Century, Germany
Silver Plate; [largest] 4" (10 cm)

# Metal

From simple, plier-like forms to highly elaborate specimens, metal nutcrackers reflect the unique qualities and limitations of metals as well as advances in metalworking production methods.

Bronze | The oldest known metal nutcracker dates to the third or fourth century B.C. and is made of bronze with gold accents. Bronze, an alloy of copper and tin, had been used hundreds of years previously for figural works.

Wrought Iron | Many nutcrackers have been created by blacksmiths in Europe and the United States over the past several centuries. The Les Secq des Tournelles Museum of Rouen, France, displays an impressive collection of hand wrought iron nutcrackers, some dating back to the 13th century.

Cast Iron | Unlike wrought iron, which is created when a blacksmith hand forges a piece of iron into a product, cast iron is created when hot iron is poured into a mold. Once a mold is made, it is easy to make a large number of items with little effort. During the 19th and 20th centuries, cast iron nutcrackers were produced in abundance both in the United States and in Europe. These included small hand lever nutcrackers as well as large, heavy tabletop models.

*Lever with Salamander Head*
Late 16th/Early 17th Century, France
Iron; 5" (12.5 cm)

Brass | Brass, an alloy of zinc and copper, has been used since biblical times. Although a few hand wrought brass nutcrackers exist, most are molded. With brass, as with bronze, it is easy to obtain a sharp image, so many highly decorated nutcrackers have emerged from molds.

England became the leader of brass products during the 19th and 20th centuries, and numerous nutcrackers were introduced. Brass was readily accepted because of its beautiful color that retains its sheen.

Silver and Metal Plate | Silver is occasionally used for nutcrackers, but because the metal is softer than brass, the shape may be damaged with extended usage. Therefore, many nutcrackers from the 18th century to present day are silver plated over brass or iron. Others have sterling handles and silver plate on the cracking mechanism. To make a more affordable nutcracker, many were plated with nickel, which gave the appearance of silver.

*To test the makeup of a plated nutcracker, a magnet can be used.
A magnet will cling to iron and steel, but will not hold to silver, brass,
bronze, or aluminum.*

mysterious

# wooden lever nutcrackers

*Gentleman of the Court*
17th Century, France
Boxwood; 10.25" (26 cm)

For a period of time spanning several centuries, the making of nutcrackers was both an art and a personal passion. The slower pace of life enabled people to invest a great deal of time and care into creating beautiful objects. Hence, common articles such as nutcrackers were highly decorated, with detailed ornamentation carefully placed to avoid interfering with the utility of the tool.

> *Their carvings reflected the period in which they worked.*

By the 15th and 16th centuries, carvers in France and England were creating beautiful wooden nutcrackers. Boxwood was their favorite wood, but fruitwood, maple, walnut, lignum vitae, and yew were also used. Their carvings reflected the period in which they worked. It is amazing that so many beautifully carved nutcrackers still exist after hundreds of years, but we must remember that these specimens were made for the wealthy or noble people and, like other decorative articles, were tended carefully by the household staff.

Several centuries later, carving surged in the areas of western Austria, Switzerland, and the Tyrolean region of northern Italy. Human and animal heads such as bears, dogs, ibex, and apes appeared as lever nutcrackers. Carvings from these areas were sold in the European markets, and the demand for carved figures grew as travelers took home nutcrackers as souvenirs.

In the Gröden Valley of northern Italy, the carvers banded together after World War I under the direction of Anton Riffeser. The company was named Anri, after the first two letters of his first and last names. Many nutcrackers were shown in the company's catalogs of the 1920s and 1930s, and the typical lever nutcracker with a curved front handle became much in demand. By the middle of the century, the more colorful, wooden toy soldier nutcracker of the Erzgebirge became the sought-after collectible, and the demand for Anri nutcrackers lessened. By 1950, only a few nutcrackers of the standing type were being produced in the Gröden Valley.

Today only a few carvers exist who make nutcrackers. Lothar Junghänel of Germany's Odenwald carves nutcrackers almost exclusively, and a handful of carvers in Germany produce nutcrackers along with other figures.

*Dog*
1880, Switzerland
Beech; 4.25" (11 cm)

*Early English Yew Nutcracker*
1669, England
Yew; 4.5" (10.5 cm)

The term *treen* is often used to describe early woodenware. In Middle English, the letter "n" was sometimes used instead of "s" to form a plural noun. Hence, objects made from trees were called "treen."

*Early English Yew Nutcracker (detail)*
Intricate engravings of a swan, monkey, fox, bearded man, and several birds grace the handles. Faces adorn the ends of the handles, and the name *George Banister* is carved into the top.

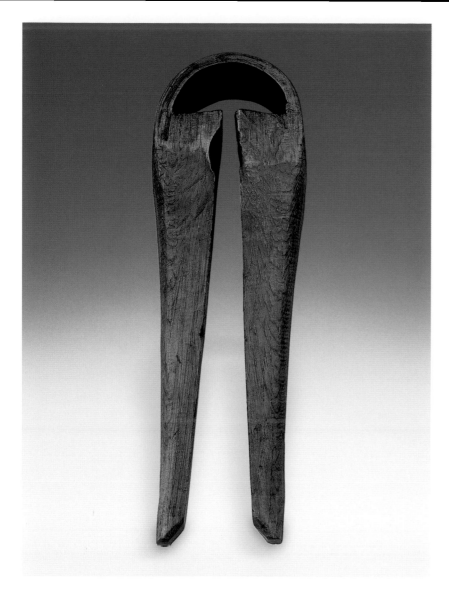

Small Pocket Crossover Lever
1788, England
Boxwood; 4" (10 cm)

*Lever Carved from Single Piece*
Late 16th/Early 17th Century, England
Ash; 6.25" (16 cm)

*Early English Lever*
Early 17th Century, England
Boxwood; 6.25" (16 cm)

*Small Pocket Crossover Lever (detail)*
This nutcracker is made of two wood pieces mortised
together with a wooden dowel. The date *1788* is
engraved on one side, and the initials *A.F.* are on the
other side.

*Folk Craft Nutcrackers*
18th Century, Europe
[top] Oak, 11.25" (28.5 cm); [left] Fruitwood, 9" (23 cm);
[right] Beech, 11" (28 cm)

*Chip-Carved Crossover Lever*
1769, England
Fruitwood; 6" (15.5 cm)

*Nutcracker with Independent Levers*
Late 18th Century, England
Fruitwood; 6.75" (17 cm)

*Crossover Levers*
17th/18th Century, England
Deciduous Wood;
[top] 6.5" (16.5 cm); [left] 5.5" (14 cm);
[right] 6.75" (17 cm); [bottom] 6.75" (17 cm)

*Decorative Lever*
17th Century, France
Fruitwood; 8.25" (21 cm)

*Carved Head on Crossover Lever*
18th Century, England
Fruitwood; 5.5" (14 cm)

11

*King Francis I*
1569, France
Boxwood; 11" (28 cm)

*King Francis I (profile)*
This exquisitely carved nutcracker depicts King Francis I of France, remembered for his generous patronage of the arts. Intricate guilloche decorations and carved ivory add to the beauty of the handles.

*King Francis I:*
*18th Century Copy of the 16th Century Original*
18th Century, France
Boxwood; 11.5" (29 cm)

*Alsace Lever Nutcrackers*
18th Century, France (Alsace Region)
Boxwood; [from left to right] 8.25" (21 cm);
8.75" (22 cm); 8" (20.5 cm); 7.5" (19 cm)

*Lever Nutcracker*
18th Century, England
Rosewood; 6" (15 cm)

*Male Figure with Initials, W.D.*
1708, England
Boxwood; 7" (17.5 cm)

*Alsace Gentleman with Wig*
18th Century, France (Alsace Region)
Fruitwood; 8.5" (21.5 cm)

*Praying Woman*
18th Century, France or Italy
Conifer; 14" (35.5 cm)

*Typical English Carving: Head of Man*
17th Century, England
Boxwood; 8.25" (21 cm)

*Court Jester with Ogre Gargoyle*
16th Century, France
Boxwood; 11.5" (29 cm)

*Praying Woman (detail)*
This large carving depicts a young woman
with hands in praying position. Both levers end
in a spiral and have a line of engraved flowers
running down the front.

*English Knight*
1692, England
Boxwood; 4.5" (11.5 cm)

*French Woman*
1650, France
Olive Tree Root; 8.25" (21 cm)

*Buccaneer with Ivory Inset*
17th Century, France
Boxwood; 8.75" (22.5 cm)

*Buccaneer with Ivory Inset (detail)*
Embedded precious stones and pieces of ivory
form a geometric pattern to decorate the midsection
of this buccaneer.

*Men from Alsace*
17th Century, France
Boxwood;
[left] 10" (25.5 cm); [right] 9.5" (24 cm)

*Monk and Asian Figure*
Late 18th Century, France
Deciduous Wood;
[left] 8.5" (21.5 cm); [right] 8" (20.5 cm)

*Boy Eating Nuts*
18th Century, France
Boxwood; 10.5" (26.5 cm)

*Turkish Man*
1770, France
Boxwood; 10.25" (26 cm)

When wood is exposed to light and air, oxidation causes it to develop a rich patina. Further, old wood is much lighter in weight, as it loses its natural moisture over time.

*Boy Eating Nuts (detail)*
The little boy stands on a pedestal, nonchalantly eating a nut from his bag. The front lever is beautifully carved in a floral decoration.

*Man with Beard*
17th Century, England
Boxwood; 8" (20.5 cm)

*Large Male Face*
18th Century, France
Boxwood; 11" (28 cm)

*Richly Patterned Galleon Design*
17th Century, England
Boxwood; 8.25" (21 cm)

*Man with Interesting Hat and Mantle*
1600, France
Boxwood; 8.5" (21.5 cm)

*Elderly French Woman*
17th Century, France
Boxwood; 7.5" (19 cm)

*Young Man Carrying Nut*
Late 17th Century, Holland
Boxwood; 5.75" (14.5 cm)

*Young Man Carrying Nut (face detail)*
Inset glass eyes accent the face of this mischievous,
curly haired young man holding a treasured acorn.

*Young Man Carrying Nut (back detail)*
Simple, flower-shaped engravings grace the back
of this lever.

*Man Holding Nut*
Late 17th/Early 18th Century, Holland
Boxwood; 5.5" (14 cm)

*Man Holding Nut (detail)*
Perhaps this elegantly dressed man was carved by
the same artist who produced the young man above.
Note the similarity in the hands.

*Three-Legged Man*
17th Century, England
Boxwood; 6" (15 cm)

*Three-Legged Man (profile)*
The handle of this nutcracker is carved in the peculiar form of a third leg that faces away from the body. In addition to helping the figure stand, the third leg could also be used as a pipe tamper.

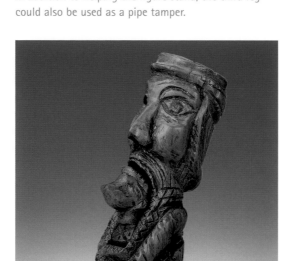

*Three-Legged Man (face detail)*
The oversized eyes, nose, and chin give this man a grotesque appearance.

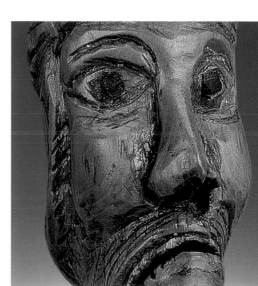

*Traditional English Carvings*
17th Century, England
Oak; [left] 5" (12.5 cm); [right] 5.5" (14 cm)

*Nude Male*
Late 17th Century, England
Boxwood; 6" (15 cm)

*Nude Male (profile)*
This nutcracker features a more primitive carving style and an oddly shaped lever.

*Monk Cradling Lamb*
17th/18th Century, France
Boxwood; 6.75" (17 cm)

*Monk Cradling Lamb (back view)*
The handle is an integrated part of the sculpture and continues the stipple detailing of the cape and hood.

*Monk Cradling Lamb (enlargement)*
Amazing detail is shown in the face, beard, and robe, as well as the hands that gently cradle the lamb.

*Monk with Metal-Lined Mouth*
17th Century, France
Boxwood; 7.25" (18.5 cm)

*Male Figure*
Late 17th/Early 18th Century, England
Boxwood; 6" (15 cm)

*Male Figure (lever detail)*
A small, delicately carved face accentuates the
handle of this nutcracker, which could also be used
as a pipe tamper.

*King with Griffin Crest*
Early 18th Century, England
Boxwood; 8" (20.5 cm)

*Gentleman of the Court*
17th Century, France
Boxwood; 10.25" (26 cm)

*Bearded Monk*
Late 17th/Early 18th Century, France or Germany
Walnut; 9.5" (24 cm)

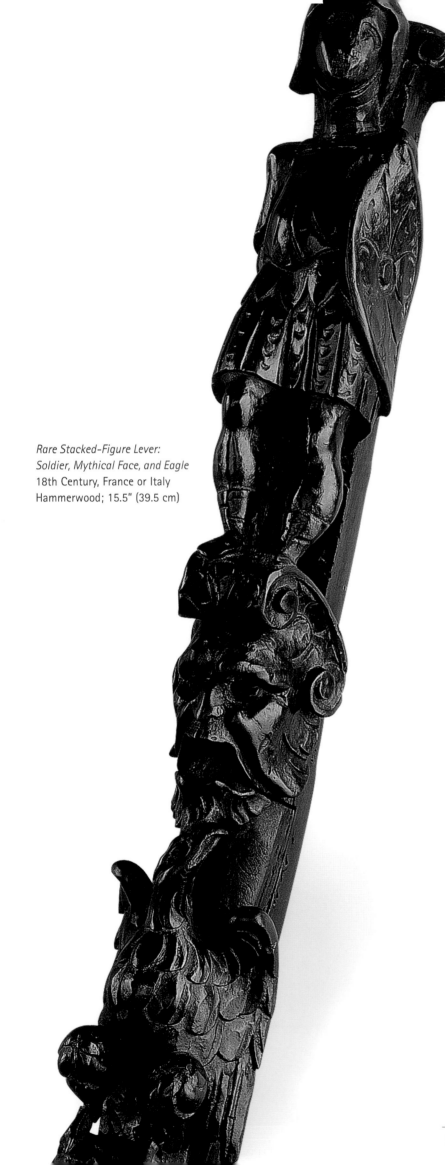

*Rare Stacked-Figure Lever:*
*Soldier, Mythical Face, and Eagle*
18th Century, France or Italy
Hammerwood; 15.5" (39.5 cm)

*Rare Stacked-Figure Lever (details)*
This nutcracker is unique, both for its extreme size and
complexity of subject matter. The ancient soldier stands
upon the angry face of a mythical god, both of which
are supported by an imposing eagle carving.

*Mythical Figure*
Early 18th Century, Italy
Walnut; 14.5" (37 cm)
*(Figure has wings instead of arms.)*

*Boy Holding Orb*
18th Century, France or Italy
Ebony; 7.5" (19 cm)

*Boy Holding Orb (detail)*
This exquisite carving mirrors classic statuary in both form and pose, and the ebony mimics a dark, polished marble. Hinged at the waist, nuts are cracked in the belly of this lever nutcracker.

*Mythical Figure (detail)*
In addition to decorative scrolls and patterns, the handle bears a secondary face below the hinge mechanism. This particular lever has hollows to accommodate small and large nuts.

*Bird*
Late 17th Century, Holland
Boxwood; 6" (15.5 cm)

*Merman*
17th Century, England
Boxwood; 6" (15.5 cm)

*Merman (side view)*
Beneath decorative aquatic scales, the tail on this unusual figure lifts to open the nutcracker. Engraved prominently on the torso are the initials *A.S.*

*Eagle*
Late 17th/Early 18th Century, England
Boxwood; 7" (18 cm)

*Squirrel*
17th Century, Italy
Oak; 11" (28 cm)

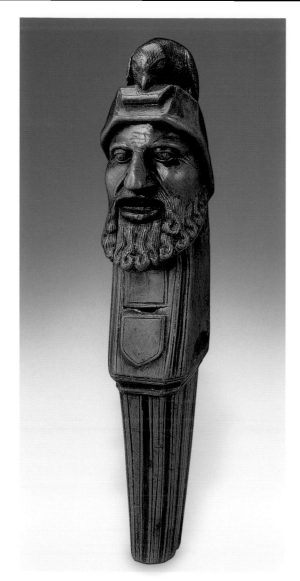

*Man with Bird on Hat*
1560–1580, France
Boxwood; 9.5" (24 cm)

*Man with Bird on Hat (detail)*
This nutcracker has a whistle in each handle. Nuts were a delicacy eaten at the end of the meal, and the whistles were probably used to call the servants.

*Monk with Long Cape and Turban*
17th Century, England
Boxwood; 8" (20.5 cm)

*Medici Family Guard with Ivory Eyes*
17th Century, Italy
Ebony; 11" (28 cm)

*Old Woman Caricature*
18th Century, France
Boxwood; 6.5" (16.5 cm)

*Elderly Woman with Child*
18th Century, Germany (Southern Region)
Mixed Materials; 8.5" (21.5 cm)

As the stylistic emphasis shifted from ornate tools to lifelike utilitarian figures, many wooden lever nutcrackers were designed with a hollowed place between the handles in the back of the figure where the nut was actually cracked. This kept the handsomely carved faces from being damaged.

*Elderly Woman with Child (detail)*
Heavy paint and shallow carvings compose the features of this folk art nutcracker that opens when the baby is lifted. A blacksmith's wrought iron was utilized during a later arm repair.

Spanish Soldier
18th Century, Italy (Gröden Valley)
Pine; 10.25" (26 cm)

Gröden Nutcrackers with Original Polychrome Paint
18th Century, Italy (Gröden Valley)
Pine; [from left to right] 7.75" (20 cm);
8.75" (22 cm); 7.5" (19.5 cm)

Early Gröden Nutcrackers
18th Century, Italy (Gröden Valley)
[from left to right] Pine, 7" (18 cm); Pine/Chestnut, 9.25" (23.5 cm);
Chestnut, 7.25" (18.5 cm)

Sailor
Late 18th Century, Italy (Gröden Valley)
Pine; 10.75" (27.5 cm)

expressive

*Lever with Silver Spring*
1879, England
Ash; 5.25" (13.5 cm)

*Lever with Silver Spring (detail)*
On one side is inscribed the initials *A* and *D*, while the other side
gives the date of *1879*.

*Levers for Pine Nuts*
19th Century, Spain
Ash; [left] 5" (12.5 cm); [front] 5" (12.5 cm);
[back] 3.75" (9.5 cm); [right] 5" (12.5 cm)

*Chip-Carved Nutcrackers*
Middle 20th Century, Yugoslavia
Various Wood Types;
[largest] 8" (20.5 cm)

*Squirrels*
19th Century, Switzerland
Conifer; [largest] 4.5" (11.5 cm)

*Long-Tailed Squirrels*
Middle 20th Century, Germany
[left] Walnut; 8" (20.5 cm); [right] Olive; 7.5" (19 cm)

*Dog and Squirrel with Glass Eyes*
Early 20th Century, Germany
Deciduous Wood;
[tallest] 3" (7.5 cm)
*(carved to lie horizontally)*

*Anri Parrot and Squirrel*
Early 20th Century, Italy (Gröden Valley)
Cembra Pine;
[tallest] 4.5" (11.5 cm)

*Chamois and Bear with Glass Eyes*
19th Century, France
Deciduous Wood;
[tallest] 3.25" (8 cm)
*(carved to lie horizontally)*

*A Whimsical Group:*
*Fox, Horse, Kissing Couple, Dog, and Female Athlete*
Early 19th Century
England (Horse and Athlete); Spain (Fox and Couple); France (Dog)
Various Wood Types; [largest] 7" (18 cm)

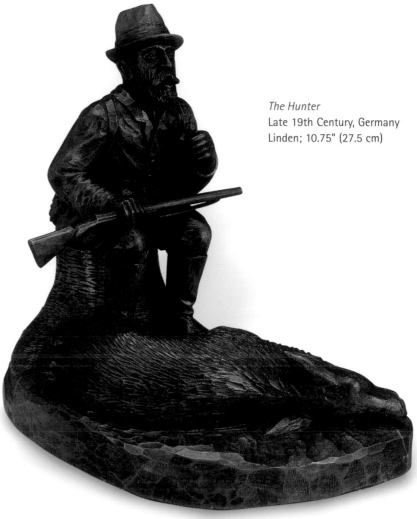

*The Hunter*
Late 19th Century, Germany
Linden; 10.75" (27.5 cm)

*Bird with Glass Eyes*
Late 19th Century, England
Linden; [height] 2.75" (7 cm)

*Animal Levers*
Early to Middle 20th Century
[back] Germany; [middle and front] Spain
Various Wood Types; [tallest] 5.5" (14 cm)

*Dog with Leather Collar,
Ivory Teeth, and Glass Eyes*
1890, Switzerland
Conifer; 9.5" (24 cm)

*Dog Howling at the Moon*
19th Century, France
Lime Wood; 7" (18 cm)

*Lever with Terrier Face (Self-Standing)*
Early 20th Century, Switzerland
Beech; 8.25" (21 cm)

*Dog with Unusual Cracking Mechanism*
Early 20th Century, Switzerland
Alder; 8.25" (21 cm)

*Anri Scottie Dog (Self-Standing)*
Early 20th Century, Italy (Gröden Valley)
Cembra Pine; 7.75" (19.5 cm)

*Man in the Moon*
19th Century, Switzerland
Conifer; [largest] 9" (23 cm)
*(Dog Figure from previous page)*

*Canine Bust with Glass Eyes*
19th Century, Switzerland
Conifer; 4.75" (12 cm)

*Meier Carvings:*
*Dog, Horse, and Seal*
1995, Germany (Altenau/Harz Mountains)
Linden; [largest] 10.75" (27.5 cm)

Animal Heads
19th/20th Century, Switzerland
Various Wood Types;
[tallest] 8.25" (21 cm)

Swiss catalogs from the late 19th and early 20th centuries pictured many carved animal nutcrackers. These were popular tourist items and hundreds were brought back to the United States as souvenirs.

Squirrel
19th Century, Switzerland
Conifer; 7" (18 cm)

Mother Bear
Late 19th Century, Switzerland
Beech; 6.25" (16 cm)

*Double Bear Nutcracker*
Early 20th Century, Switzerland
Conifer; 8.25" (21 cm)

*Double Bear Nutcracker (detail)*
Truly a man's nutcracker—the wide grip of the
handles matches the strong and powerful arms and
paws of the bear.

*A Bear Convention*
Late 19th/Early 20th Century, Switzerland
Various Wood Types; [largest] 9.5" (24 cm);
[smallest] 5.25" (13.5 cm)

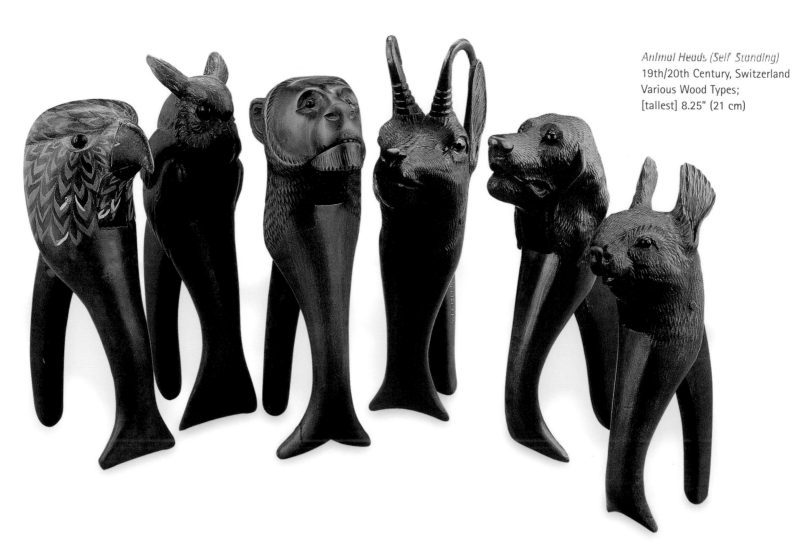

Animal Heads (Self Standing)
19th/20th Century, Switzerland
Various Wood Types;
[tallest] 8.25" (21 cm)

Raven (Made for International Convention)
Late 19th Century, France
Deciduous Wood; 9.5" (24 cm)

Exceptional Bird Carvings
1860, Switzerland
Beech; [largest] 8.5" (21.5 cm)

Owl
Early 20th Century, France
Conifer; 7.5" (19 cm)

Owl (detail)
This is an unusual cracking method as the owl
itself serves as the handle to raise and lower the book,
which cracks the nut.

Monkey Holding His Tail
Early 20th Century, Germany
Conifer; 11.25" (28.5 cm)

Ape with Glass Eyes
1860, Switzerland
Beech; 6.75" (17 cm)

*Gorilla with Glass Eyes*
19th Century, Switzerland
Fruitwood; 4.75" (12 cm)

*Gorilla with Glass Eyes (detail)*
Natural-looking glass eyes are inserted in many figural nutcrackers to make them more appealing to the collector.

*Lion, Dog, and Bear (Half-Bodied Figures with Glass Eyes)*
1880, Switzerland
Various Wood Types; [from left to right] 4.25" (11 cm);
4.25" (11 cm); 4.5" (11.5 cm)

*Cat and Dog (Made for International Convention)*
Late 19th Century, France
Deciduous Wood;
[largest] 10" (25.5 cm)

*Animal Figures in Formal Attire*
1880, Switzerland
Beech; [from left to right] 7" (18 cm);
7" (18 cm); 6.5" (16.5 cm)

*Early Anri Figures:*
*Cat, Frog, and Mouse*
Early 20th Century, Italy (Gröden Valley)
Cembra Pine; [tallest] 5.5" (14 cm)

*Bird (Cracks Nut in Beak)*
Early 20th Century, Germany
Conifer; 11.25" (28.5 cm)

*Anri Animals*
Early 20th Century, Italy (Gröden Valley)
Cembra Pine; [tallest] 8.5" (21.5 cm)

*Carved Animal Shapes*
Middle to Late 20th Century, Germany (Rhön)
Linden; [from left to right] 8.5" (21.5 cm); 7" (18 cm);
10.25" (26 cm); 6.25" (16 cm)

*Colorful Bird*
1920, Germany (Southern Region)
Conifer; 9.25" (23.5 cm)

Crocodile Chasing Boy
20th Century, United States
Unknown Wood Type; 8.75" (22.5 cm)

Modernistic Crocodile Head (Cracks Nut in Jaws)
1930, France
Deciduous Wood; [height] 2.75" (7 cm)

A Real Nut "Quacker"
Late 20th Century, Canada
Oak; 7.75" (20 cm)

Chubby Parrots
20th Century, Denmark
Beech; [chick] 6.25" (16 cm); [adult] 10.5" (26 cm)

*Carved Shoe*
Middle 20th Century, Holland
Maple; [height] 3" (7.5 cm)

*Grand Ibex Head*
Middle 20th Century, Switzerland
Beech; 12" (30.5 cm)

*Butting Heads (Rams)*
2003, Germany
Linden; 6.75" (17 cm)
*(carved by Matthias Freund)*

*Beer Wagon*
2003, Germany
Linden; 7" (18 cm)
*(carved by Matthias Freund)*

*Beer Wagon (detail)*
The top row of barrels is hinged to make a lever, and the nut is cracked between the top and middle rows.

*Cheese and Mouse*
2003, Germany
Linden; 5.5" (14 cm)
*(carved by Matthias Freund)*

*Happy Couple*
19th Century, Switzerland
Conifer; 9.25" (23.5 cm)

*Happy Couple (detail)*
A romantic pair who kiss each time the nutcracker is used.

*A Variety of Carved Heads*
Late 19th/Early 20th Century, France and Switzerland
Various Wood Types; [largest] 8.5" (21.5 cm)

*African Caricature*
1980, Germany
Walnut; 10.5" (26.5 cm)

*Madman (with Unusual Cracking Device)*
Late 19th/Early 20th Century, Switzerland
Beech; 6.75" (17 cm)

*Contorted Faces*
1860, France
Walnut; [female] 9" (23 cm); [male] 9.25" (23.5 cm)

*Group of Sitting Gnomes*
Late 19th Century, Switzerland
Various Wood Types;
[from left to right] 9" (23 cm); 10.75" (27.5 cm);
10.5" (26.5 cm); 8.5" (21.5 cm)

*Music Box (with Humorous Male Face)*
Late 19th Century, Switzerland
Conifer; [height] 6" (15.5 cm)
*(When the nose is lifted to crack a nut, the music box begins playing.)*

*A Trio of Expressive Figures*
19th Century, Switzerland
Walnut; [tallest] 4" (10 cm)

*Reversible Head*
19th Century, Switzerland
Walnut; 5" (13 cm)

*Reversible Head (detail)*
This fascinating nutcracker shows a different face
as it is turned upside down. The long hat brims are
lifted to reveal the nut receptacle.

*Male Bust*
2000, Germany (Altenau/Harz Mountains)
Linden; 6.75" (17 cm)
*(carved by Meier)*

*Seated Man with Long Nose*
Early 20th Century, Belgium
Deciduous Wood; 11.25" (28.5 cm)

*Spanish Soldier*
Late 19th Century, Switzerland
Conifer; 5" (13 cm)
*(This is a copy of a nutcracker originally created in the 17th century.)*

*Group of Women*
19th Century, Switzerland
Conifer; [largest] 8" (20.5 cm)

*Female Torso*
1880, Switzerland
Conifer; 6.25" (16 cm)

*Bretons*
Early 20th Century, France
Oak; [largest] 7.25" (18.5 cm)

*Farmer and Wife*
19th Century, Switzerland
Conifer; [largest] 6.75" (17 cm)

*Men and Women*
(Made for International Convention in Paris)
Late 19th Century, France
Deciduous Wood;
[largest] 10.25" (26 cm)

*Forest Gnome*
Late 19th Century, Switzerland
Deciduous Wood; 9" (23 cm)

*Joker*
1880, Belgium
Deciduous Wood; 8" (20.5 cm)

*Jovial Gentlemen*
Late19th/Early 20th Century, Switzerland
Linden; [from left to right] 8.25" (21 cm); 8.25" (21 cm);
9" (23 cm); 8.25" (21 cm)

*Military Figures*
19th Century, Switzerland
Deciduous Wood; [left] 8" (20.5 cm); [right] 8.25" (21 cm)

*General Ulysses S. Grant, Emperor Wilhelm II,
and King Louis Philippe*
19th Century, France
Beech; [largest] 9" (23 cm)

*A Fox and Gnomes in Tree Trunks*
Late 19th Century, Switzerland
Conifer; [height, clockwise from left] 4.75" (12 cm);
4.25" (11 cm); 3" (7.5 cm)

*Finely Carved Gentleman (with Movable Arms)*
19th Century, Switzerland
Beech; 8.5" (21.5 cm)

*Farmer's Wife*
19th Century, France
Boxwood; 7" (18 cm)

*Several Distinctive Fellows*
1900, France
Boxwood; [from left to right] 8" (20.5 cm); 8.25" (21 cm); 8.25" (21 cm); 9" (23 cm); 8.5" (21.5 cm)

*Gentlemen with Hats*
Late 19th Century, France
Boxwood;
[tallest] 8" (20.5 cm)

*Stylized Male Figures*
1930, Denmark
[left] Teak, 7.5" (19 cm); [right] Beech, 8.5" (21.5 cm)
*(right-hand figure carved by Kay Boesen)*

*Kinq*
Late 20th Century, Germany
Linden; 16" (40.5 cm)
*(carved by Weichelt)*

*Assorted Group of Little People*
19th Century, Switzerland
Conifer; [tallest] 7.25" (18.5 cm)

*A Motley Crew*
Middle to Late 19th Century, Switzerland
Conifer; [from left to right] 6.5" (16.5 cm); 6.75" (17 cm);
7.5" (19 cm); 6.75" (17 cm)

*Grotesque Levers*
1980, Austria
Linden; [left] 7" (18 cm); [back] 10.5" (26.5 cm);
[front] 2.5" (6.5 cm)

*Smiling Figure with Rosy Cheeks*
1930, Germany
Beech; 10.5" (26.5 cm)

*An International Group*
20th Century, Germany
Various Wood Types; [largest] 15.5" (39.5 cm);
[smallest] 9" (23 cm)

*Unique Gnome*
1920, Germany
Deciduous Wood; [height] 6.75" (17 cm)
*(Nut is cracked under the belly.)*

*Folk Art*
[left] 1930, Germany; [right] Date and Origin Unknown
[from left to right] Linden/Walnut, 14" (35.5 cm); Beech, 14.5" (37 cm)
*(Note the number of fingers and toes on the right-hand figure.)*

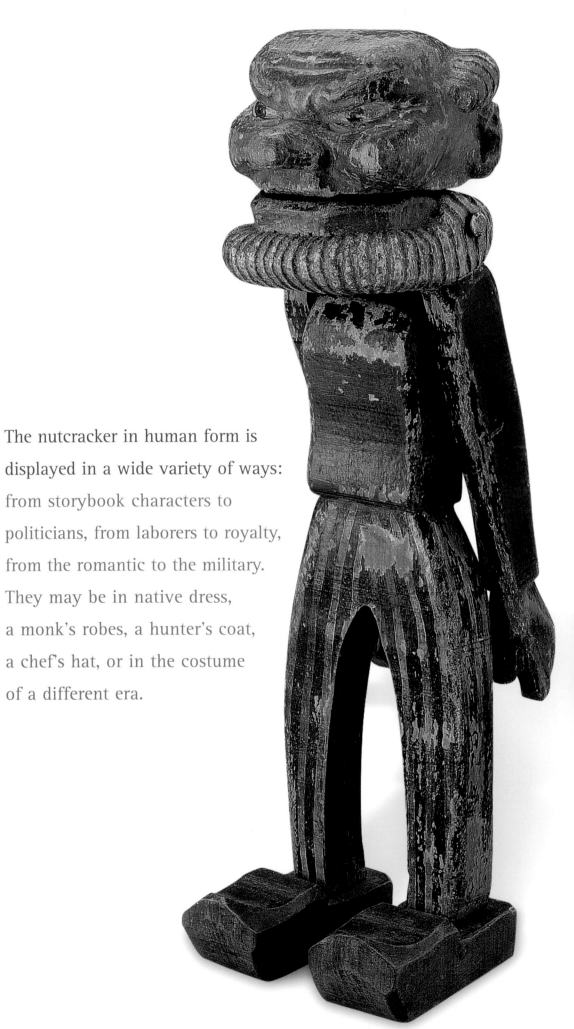

The nutcracker in human form is displayed in a wide variety of ways: from storybook characters to politicians, from laborers to royalty, from the romantic to the military. They may be in native dress, a monk's robes, a hunter's coat, a chef's hat, or in the costume of a different era.

*Dutch Character*
1850, Germany (Southern Region)
Conifer; 14.5" (37 cm)

*Dutch Character (detail)*
This has an unusual working mechanism as the mouth opens when the arms are lifted backward (behind the body).

*Finely Carved Man's Face*
Late 19th/Early 20th Century, Origin Unknown
Beech; 9.5" (24 cm)
*(A hinge on top of the head allows the lever to open.)*

*Russian Figures*
[natural] Early 20th Century, Russia; [painted] Late 20th Century, Russia
Linden; [from left to right] 8" (20.5 cm); 14.25" (36.5 cm);
11.5" (29 cm)

*Anri Characters (Self-Standing)*
Early 20th Century, Italy (Gröden Valley)
Cembra Pine;
[tallest] 8" (20.5 cm)

*Norwegian Folk*
20th Century, Norway
Conifer;
[from left to right] 7.75" (19.5 cm); 7.75" (19.5 cm);
8.75" (22 cm); 8.25" (21 cm)

*Norsemen*
20th Century, Norway
Conifer;
[from left to right] 8.5" (21.5 cm); 8.75" (22 cm); 8" (20.5 cm)

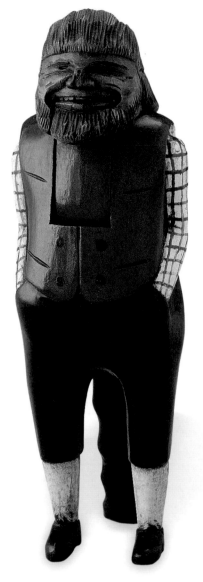

*Werewolf*
1920, Switzerland
Walnut; 8.5" (21.5 cm)

*Rare, Interesting, and Uncommon Characters*
1930, Germany
Beech; [tallest] 9.75" (25 cm)
*(carved in Munich by Göttlich)*

*Men with Long-Brimmed Hats*
1910, Germany
Conifer; [left] 7" (18 cm); [right] 9.25" (23.5 cm)

*Like Father: Innkeeper*
1940, Germany (Erzgebirge)
Linden; 9.5" (24 cm)
*(carved by Hans Hanig)*

*Like Son: Hunter*
1980, Germany (Erzgebirge)
Linden; 11" (28 cm)
*(carved by Jost Hanig, Hans's son)*

*Indian Palace Guard*
Early 19th Century, Germany
Oak; 15.25" (38 cm)

*Indian Palace Guard (detail)*
Nuts are cracked beneath the brightly colored
head scarf of this unusual figure.

*Hunter, Bavarian, and Pirate*
1980, Spain
Deciduous Wood; [all figures] 14.75" (37.5 cm)

*Man with Long Nose*
Late 20th Century, Germany
Conifer; 13.25" (33.5 cm)

intricate

# wooden screw nutcrackers

Lever nutcrackers preceded the screw type by centuries, as screw nutcrackers were not introduced until the 17th century. Most of the early screw nutcrackers were simple in design, but with a variety of woods such as boxwood, maple, fruitwood, and yew. Some had ivory and ebony trim.

> *Most of the early screw nutcrackers were simple in design.*

The full-figured screw nutcrackers usually had the cavity for the nut at the back of the chest, while the lower part of the body, legs, and feet connected to the screw part. When only heads of animals or humans were used, the cavity opened into the back of the head, and a handle operated the screw mechanism.

While folk artists have continued to paint designs on simple, turned, wooden barrel-screw nutcrackers, European carvers have produced highly elaborate screw nutcrackers with figures of humans and animals.

*Cobnut Screw*
Early 18th Century, England
Boxwood; 3.5" (8.5 cm)

*Simple Screws*
Early 19th Century, France
Boxwood; [largest] 5.5" (14 cm);
[smallest] 4.5" (11.5 cm)

*Humpbacked Man*
19th Century, France
Beech; 6.75" (17 cm)

*Pocket Screws*
18th Century, England
Various Wood Types;
[largest] 4.75" (12 cm); [smallest] 2.75" (7 cm)

*Cobnut Screw*
Early 18th Century, England
Boxwood; 3.5" (8.5 cm)

*Lion*
18th Century, France
Walnut; 6.75" (17 cm)

*Lion Bust*
18th Century, Switzerland
Beech; 5.75" (14.5 cm)

*Lion Bust* (detail)
A majestic lion with long mane, powerful jaws, and fierce, protruding fangs.

*Smiling Woman with Infant*
Late 18th Century, France
Walnut; 6.5" (16.5 cm)

*Smiling Woman with Infant* (detail)
Perhaps this woman is singing a lullaby as she gently holds the infant in her hands. The screw mechanism which cracks the nut also serves as a stool upon which the woman sits.

The screw mechanism allows pressure to be added gradually until the nut is cracked. This controlled method results in more whole kernels than the lever method, which applies a more forceful impact.

*Seated Man*
18th Century, France
Walnut; 7.25" (18.5 cm)

*Man with Pipe*
Late 18th Century, France
Boxwood; 8.5" (21.5 cm)

*Seated Man (detail)*
The nut is placed in the chest cavity and is cracked as the handle turns and the screw presses toward the chin.

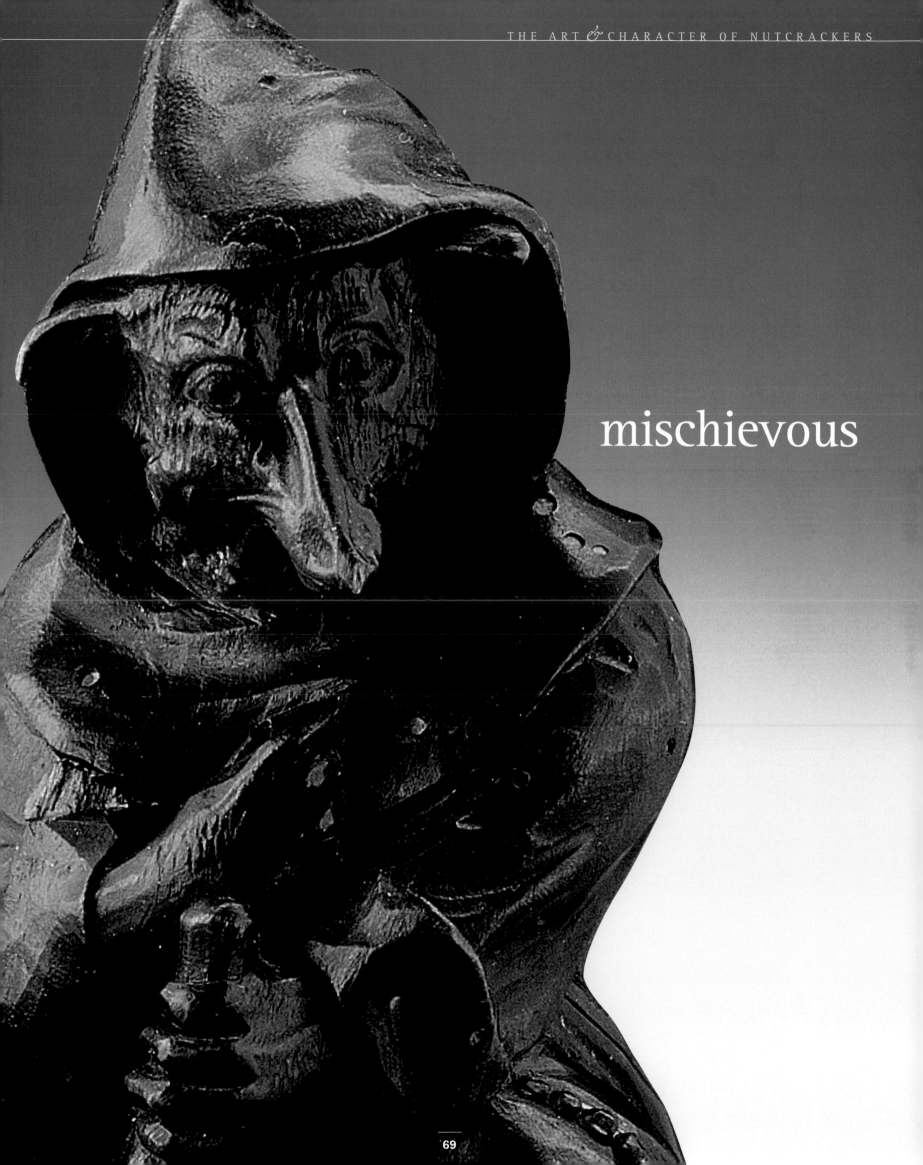

mischievous

*Diverse Group of Screw Nutcrackers*
19th Century, France
Boxwood, Maple, Ebony; [tallest] 6.5" (16.5 cm)
*(Some feature ivory trim.)*

*Ring Screw*
1890, Scandinavia
Conifer; 3.75" (9.5 cm)

*Dual-Aperture Nutcracker (front and back)*
Late 18th/Early 19th Century, England
Boxwood; 2.75" (7 cm)

*(separate receptacles for different sized nuts)*

*Screw with Inlaid Wood*
Early 19th Century, France
Various Wood Types; 5.5" (14 cm)

*Simple Screws*
Early 19th Century, France
Boxwood; [largest] 5.5" (14 cm);
[smallest] 4.5" (11.5 cm)

*Highly Decorative Screws*
19th Century, Switzerland (French-Speaking Region)
Deciduous Wood;
[largest] 4.25" (11 cm); [smallest] 3.5" (9 cm)

*Hazelnut Screws*
19th Century, Switzerland
Conifer;
[top] 7.25" (18.5 cm); [bottom] 6.75" (17 cm)

*Ornamental Screws*
1820 to 1880, Italy (Tyrolean Area)
Walnut;
[tallest] 9" (23 cm)

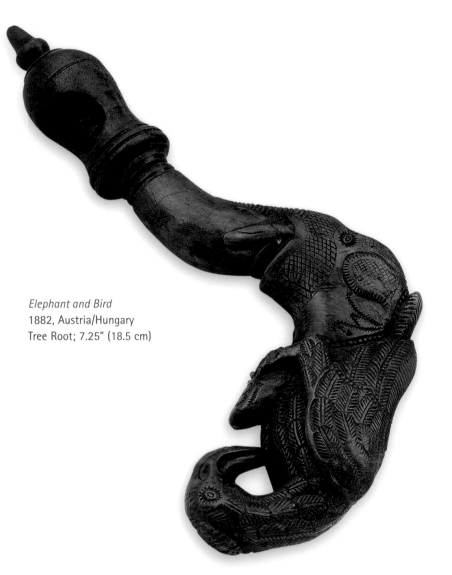

*Elephant and Bird*
1882, Austria/Hungary
Tree Root; 7.25" (18.5 cm)

*Various Fist-Shaped Screws*
19th Century, Switzerland/France
Various Wood Types;
[largest] 7.5" (19 cm); [smallest] 6" (15.5 cm)

*Elephant and Bird (detail)*
This unusual nutcracker shows an elephant's trunk
and a beautifully carved bird in full plumage.

*Head of a Dog*
1880, France
Cherry; 5" (12.5 cm)

*Unique Dog with Bone Neck*
19th Century, England
Various Wood Types/Bone; 8.5" (21.5 cm)

*A Fortunate Gentleman and an Unlucky Man*
19th Century, Switzerland
Beech; [largest] 4" (10 cm)

*A Fortunate Gentleman and an Unlucky Man (back)*
The gentleman watches as a bird settles on the head of his friend and reaches for his nose.

*Cat Head (with Glass Eyes)*
1880, England
Fruitwood; [height] 2.5" (6.5 cm)

*Dog Head*
1860, Austria/Hungary
Conifer; [height] 2.25" (6 cm)

*The Big, Bad Wolf*
19th Century, France (Alsace Region)
Walnut; 8.75" (22 cm)

*Animal Heads*
19th Century, France
Various Wood Types;
[length, from left to right]
6.5" (16.5 cm); 8.25" (21 cm);
7.75" (19.5 cm); 8" (20.5 cm);
7" (18 cm)

*Fox with Captured Bird*
Early 19th Century, France
Deciduous Wood; [height] 2.25" (6 cm)

*Crocodile, Bird, and Peacock*
19th Century, Switzerland
Walnut (crocodile and bird); Beech (peacock);
[tallest] 2.75" (7 cm)

*Three Bears*
1890, Switzerland (standing figures) and England
Various Wood Types; [largest] 5.75" (14.5 cm)

*House on the Hill and Horse with Rider*
1850, France
[left] Fruitwood; [right] Beech; [both figures] 3.5" (9 cm)

*Monkeys*
Early 19th Century, France
Walnut; [left] 6.5" (16.5 cm); [right] 7" (18 cm)

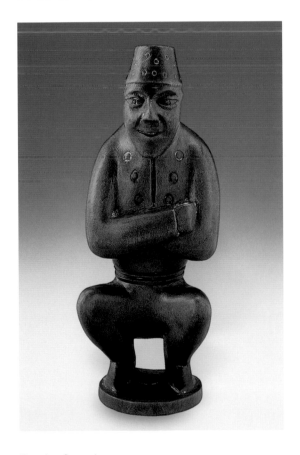

*Dancing Cossack*
19th Century, France
Boxwood; 4.75" (12 cm)

*Three Musicians*
19th Century, Italy (Gröden Valley)
Conifer; [from left to right] 6.25" (16 cm);
6.5" (16.5 cm); 5.25" (13.5 cm)

*Male and Female Musicians*
19th Century, Italy (Gröden Valley)
Conifer; [tallest] 8" (20.5 cm)

*Jolly Swashbuckler (detail)*
The carver created a humorous character with
the floppy hat, bushy beard, expressive eyes, and a
wide grin.

*Man Sitting Astride Nutcracker*
Middle 19th Century, France
Lime Wood; 9.75" (25 cm)

*Jolly Swashbuckler*
1890, Italy (Gröden Valley)
Conifer; 8.25" (21 cm)

*Man Carrying Woman*
19th Century, Switzerland
Conifer; 7" (18 cm)

*Man Carrying Woman (detail)*
We wonder how the woman got up on the man's shoulders, and where he is taking her.

*A Gathering of Noblemen*
1890, Italy (Gröden Valley)
Beech;
[largest] 9" (23 cm)

*Man Balancing on One Foot*
19th Century, Italy (Gröden Valley)
Conifer; 7.25" (18.5 cm)

*A Variety of Seated Figures*
19th Century, Italy (Gröden Valley)
Conifer; [tallest] 7.5" (19 cm)

*Shoemaker*
19th Century, Italy (Gröden Valley)
Conifer; 7.5" (19 cm)

*Humpbacked Man (detail)*
This squatting, bulbous character grins as he holds
his head in his hands.

*Humpbacked Man*
19th Century, France
Beech; 6.75" (17 cm)

*Man (with Full Sideburns)*
19th Century, France
Maple; 8" (20.5 cm)

*Double-Sided Screws*
19th Century
Various Wood Types;
[from left to right] England, 6" (15 cm);
Switzerland, 7.25" (18.5 cm); France, 6.75" (17 cm)

*Double-Sided Screws (opposite side)*
Each of these grotesque screws has mouth agape to crack the nut
and a different design on the reverse side.

*Bearded, Bald Man*
19th Century, France
Conifer; 6.25" (16 cm)
*(also featured in grouping to the right)*

*A Collection of Carved Heads*
19th Century, France
Various Wood Types; [tallest] 8" (20.5 cm)

*Wrestling Competitors*
1820, Holland
Conifer; 7" (18 cm)

*Wrestling Competitors (opposite side)*
The platform for the figures has a beautifully carved floral design. The opening for the nut is the center of a flower in full bloom.

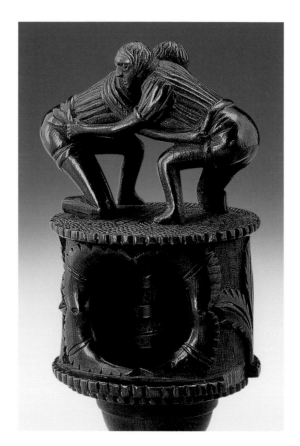

*Differing Opinions of a Seashell*
Late 19th/Early 20th Century, France/Switzerland
Various Wood Types; [tallest] 7" (18 cm)

*Soldier*
Late 18th/Early 19th Century, France
Boxwood; 7.5" (19 cm)

*Soldier (detail)*
The hat of this Napoleonic soldier is trimmed with tassels, and his shortened cape is carved to resemble wool. Note his neatly braided hair.

*Man with Pipe*
1850, Italy (Gröden Valley)
Pear Wood; 7.5" (19 cm)

*Handsome Man (with Hat) and Rosenkavalier*
Early 19th Century, England
Fruitwood; [standing] 7.25" (18.5 cm);
[front] 8.75" (22.5 cm)

*Gentleman and Clown*
Early 20th Century, Austria
Linden; 7" (18 cm)

*Prince, King, and Friar*
19th Century, Germany (Southern Region)
Linden; [tallest] 8.5" (21.5 cm)

*Colorful Folk Art Screws (detail)*
Colorful, cheerful designs decorate these interesting folk art pieces.

*Colorful Folk Art Screws*
20th Century, Austria
Conifer; [front] 6" (15.5 cm);
[from left to right] 4.5" (11.5 cm); 6.75" (17 cm);
5.75" (14.5 cm)

*Funny Faces*
20th Century, Japan
Various Wood Types; [tallest] 5.75" (14.5 cm)

*Fruit and Faces*
20th Century, Italy
Beech; [tallest] 6" (15.5 cm); [shortest] 4.25" (11 cm)

*Geometric Designs*
20th Century, Germany/China/Mexico/Spain/
United States/Romania/Austria
Various Wood Types; [largest] 7.5" (19 cm)

tidy

# wooden percussion nutcrackers

Cracking nuts with a wooden hammer and bowl is still a popular tradition during Christmas gatherings. A wooden hammer is often preferred over a metal hammer as a nut-cracking device, primarily because it is not as likely to crush the kernel.

> *Percussion nutcrackers are sometimes very humorous creations.*

Percussion nutcrackers are sometimes very humorous creations. Often the nut is cracked by hitting a human-like figure on the head. A very early figural wooden percussion nutcracker of this type is a snowman designed by Wilhelm Füchtner around 1890. The nut is placed in a cavity at the back of the figure, and the snowman is hit on the head to crack the nut. This same system is used by other wooden percussion nutcrackers.

*Erzgebirge Percussion Figures*
Late 20th Century, Germany
Various Wood Types;
[from left to right] 12" (30.5 cm); 17.5" (44.5 cm);
10.5" (26.5 cm); 9" (23 cm)

*Snowman*
1890, Germany
Linden; 10" (25.5 cm)
*(by Wilhelm Füchtner)*

*Humorous Percussion Figures*
Late 20th Century, United States
Alaskan Cedar; [Santa Claus—shown disassembled] 8.5" (21.5 cm);
[back—from left to right] 8" (20.5 cm); 10.25" (26 cm);
10.5" (27 cm); 8.25" (21 cm)

The late Jack Frost of Washington State used slow-growing Alaskan cedar for his percussion nutcrackers, as the compact growth rings made for an extremely strong, durable wood.

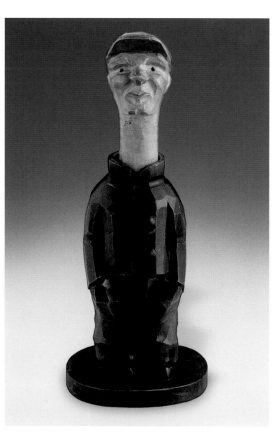

*Man with Exceptionally Long Neck*
Early 20th Century, Austria
Conifer; 8.75" (22.5 cm)

*Housewife (with Broom)*
Early 20th Century, Germany
Conifer; 12.25" (32 cm)

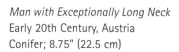

*Santa Claus*
Late 20th Century, United States
Alaskan Cedar; 8.5" (21.5 cm)
*(featured in grouping to the left)*

*Mortar and Pestle*
Late 20th Century, Africa (Tanzania)
Ebony; 4.25" (11 cm)

*Percussion Punch*
19th Century, Wales
Lignum Vitae; 6.5" (16.5 cm)

*Assorted Percussion Nutcrackers*
Various Wood Types
[front—bowl] Middle 20th Century, Japan; 2.5" (6.5 cm)
[left—punch] Patented 1953, United States; 6.75" (17 cm)
[right—block] 19th Century, United States; 4.5" (11.5 cm)
[and hammer] 8" (20.5 cm)

practical

# metal lever nutcrackers

The metal lever is the most common nutcracker type produced. Nearly every American household for the past 200 years has had one in the kitchen cupboard. First forged by blacksmiths, then molded of hot metal, lever nutcrackers are readily available today at hardware and kitchen shops, and most of them employ the direct-pressure method.

*Metal nutcrackers are shown in a variety of figural designs.*

As in wood, metal nutcrackers are shown in a variety of figural designs, from small brass hand-held levers to bulky table models of cast iron. Squirrels, because of their appetite for nuts, have been designed repeatedly. Dogs, though not nut eaters, have been made in many different breeds. One of the most intriguing metal figural designs is of an English-made kangaroo that cracks the nut in her pouch.

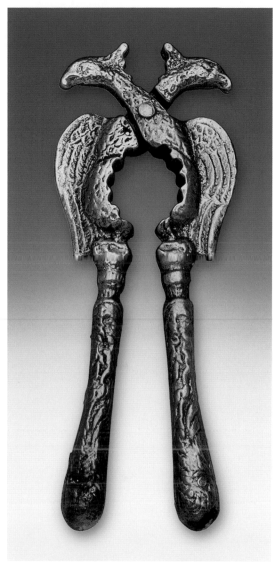

*Twin-Headed Falcon Nutcracker*
17th Century, Origin Unknown
Brass; 6" (15.5 cm)
*(recently discovered buried in Holland)*

*Simple Metal Levers*
Early 19th Century, Europe/United States
Iron; [largest] 5.75" (14.5 cm)

*Frog*
1900, France
Silver Plating/Brass; 5" (12.5 cm)

*Remarkable Brass Lever*
15th Century, France
Brass; 5" (12.5 cm)

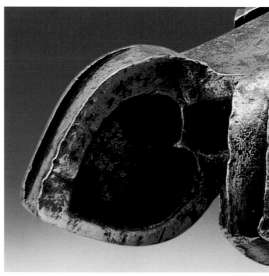

*Nutcracker with Heart-Shaped Receptacle (detail)*
This interesting hand-forged nutcracker with its heart shape may have been a gift to a loved one. Larger nuts can also be cracked between the handles.

*Nutcracker with Heart-Shaped Receptacle*
18th Century, France
Iron; 5.25" (13.5 cm)

*Iron Nutcrackers with Decorative Handles*
18th Century, France
Iron; [from left to right] 4.75" (12 cm); 5" (12.5 cm);
4.5" (11.5 cm); [front] 4.75" (12 cm)

*Nutcrackers for Small or Large Nuts*
17th Century, France
Iron/Brass; [from top to bottom] 6" (15.5 cm); 6" (15.5 cm); 5.75" (14.5 cm)

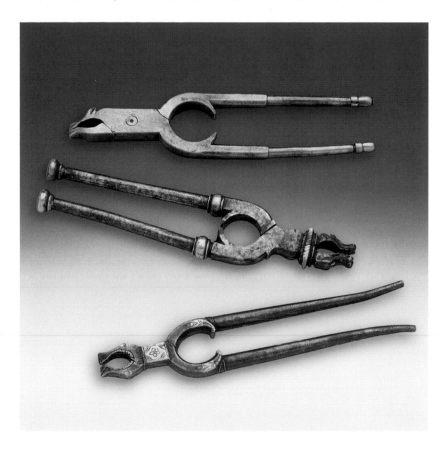

*Forged Iron Lever*
17th Century, France
Iron; 5.5" (14 cm)

*Forged Iron Lever (detail)*
A small built-in whistle at the end of one handle may
have been used to call servants to the table.

*Hand-Forged Nutcracker (for Cobnuts)*
15th Century, France
Iron; 6" (15.5 cm)

*Early Nutcracker (with Human Face)*
Late 15th/Early 16th Century, France
Iron; 5.25" (13.5 cm)

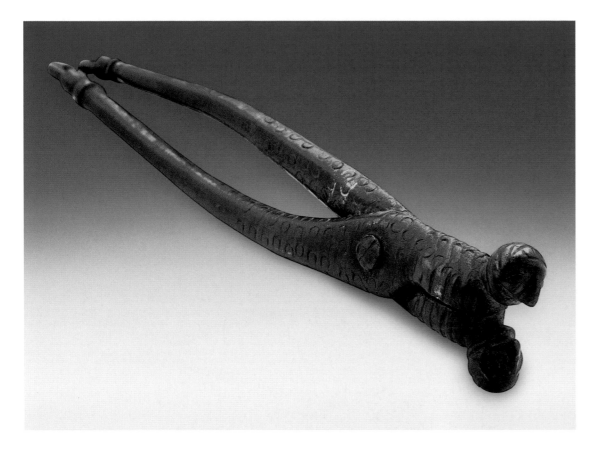

*Nutcracker for Small Nuts*
Late 17th/Early 18th Century, France
Iron; 5.5" (14 cm)

*Early Forged and Chased Plier*
16th Century, France
Iron; 7.25" (18.5 cm)

*Twin-Headed Falcon Nutcracker*
17th Century, Origin Unknown
Brass; 6" (15.5 cm)
*(recently discovered buried in Holland)*

*Remarkable Brass Nutcracker*
17th Century, France
Brass; 7" (18 cm)

*Remarkable Brass Nutcracker (detail)*
This nutcracker depicts a man held firmly in stocks. Note the elaborate detail of both front and back levers.

*Levers with Geometric Designs*
Late 16th/Early 17th Century, France
Iron; [back] 4.75" (12 cm); [front] 5" (12.5 cm)

*Levers with Geometric Designs (detail)*
This tiny nutcracker for cobnuts has the design of a star with eight points.

coy

*Plier Nutcracker Composition*
19th Century, Germany/France/England
Iron; [longest] 6" (15.5 cm)

*Nutcrackers for Large or Small Nuts*
Early 19th Century, Germany/France
Silver Plate/Iron; [largest] 6.75" (17 cm)

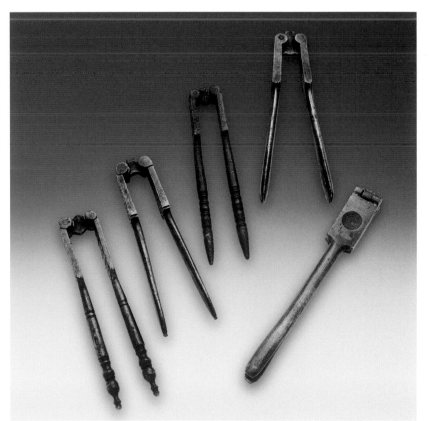

*Simple Metal Levers*
Early 19th Century, Europe/United States
Iron; [tallest] 5.75" (14.5 cm)

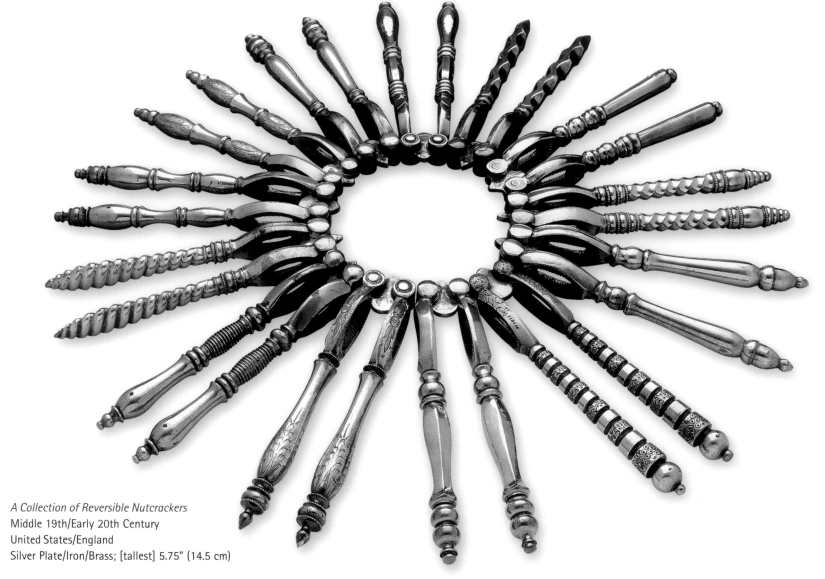

*A Collection of Reversible Nutcrackers*
Middle 19th/Early 20th Century
United States/England
Silver Plate/Iron/Brass; [tallest] 5.75" (14.5 cm)

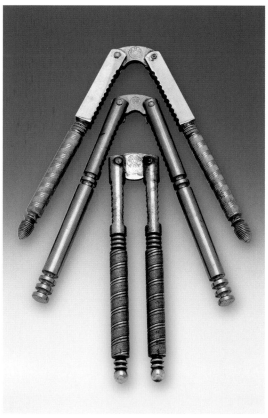

*Quackenbush Nutcrackers*
Late 19th/Early 20th Century, United States
Silver Plate/Iron; 5" (13 cm)
*(The original Quackenbush design was patented in 1889.)*

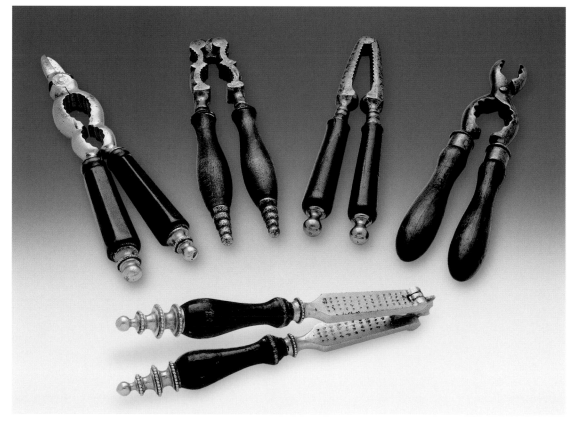

*Various Wood-Handled Nutcrackers*
19th Century, Germany/France
Iron/Wood; [largest] 7" (18 cm)
*(Several nutcrackers in this grouping have silver trim.)*

A Diverse Group of Reversible Nutcrackers
*(with Interesting Cracking Mechanisms)*
Middle 19th/Early 20th Century, United States/England
Silver Plate/Iron/Brass; [tallest] 6.25" (16 cm);
[smallest] 5.25" (13.5 cm)

*Nutcrackers for Pine Nuts*
19th Century, Spain
Brass; [left] 4" (10 cm); [right] 5" (12.5 cm)

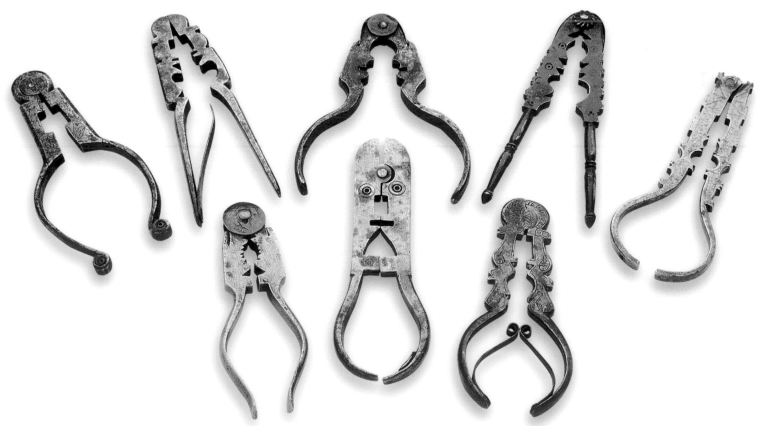

*Various Pine Nut Levers*
19th Century, Spain
Iron, [largest] 5.75" (14.5 cm); [shortest] 4" (10 cm)

*Elegant Sterling Silver Nutcrackers*
Late 19th/Early 20th Century, England/France
Sterling Silver; [tallest] 6" (15.5 cm)
(The Rothschild crest is visible on the front nutcracker's handle.)

In Victorian times, nutcrackers were included in many silver table settings, as nuts were served with fruit for dessert—hence the expression "from soup to nuts." Nearly every major silver service manufacturer included nutcrackers in its catalogs.

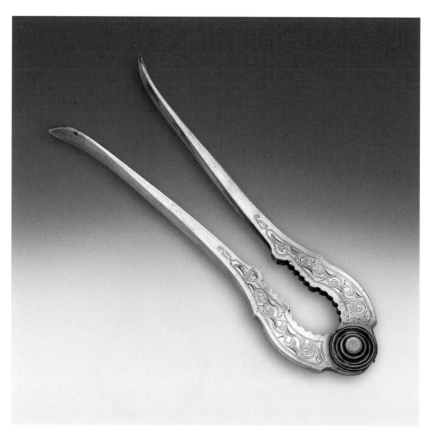

*Formal Table Nutcracker*
Early 19th Century, France
Silver Plate/Brass; 7" (18 cm)

*Reversible Nutcracker (with Grapevine Design)*
Early 20th Century, United States
Silver Plate/Brass; 5.5" (14 cm)

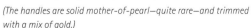

*Embellished Reversible Nutcracker*
Late 19th Century, England
Silver Plate/Iron; 5.75" (14.5 cm)

*(The handles are solid mother-of-pearl—quite rare—and trimmed with a mix of gold.)*

*Various Victorian Nutcrackers*
Middle 19th/Early 20th Century, Europe
Silver/Brass/Iron; [largest] 7.75" (19.5 cm);
[smallest] 6" (15.5 cm)

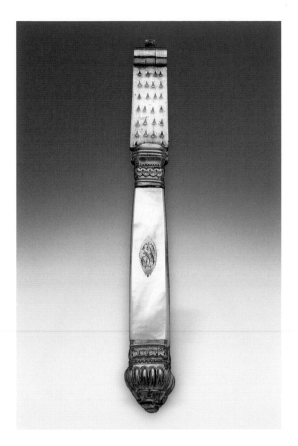

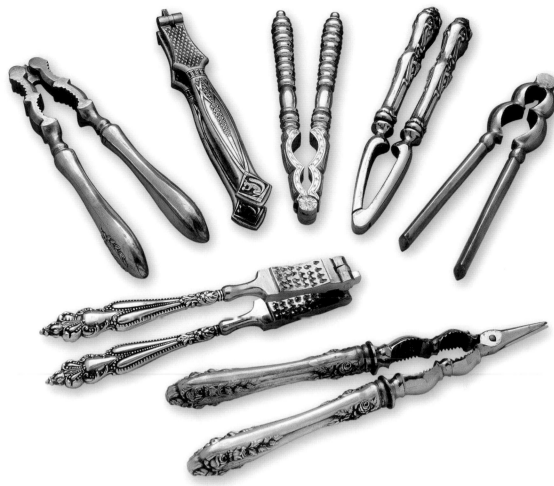

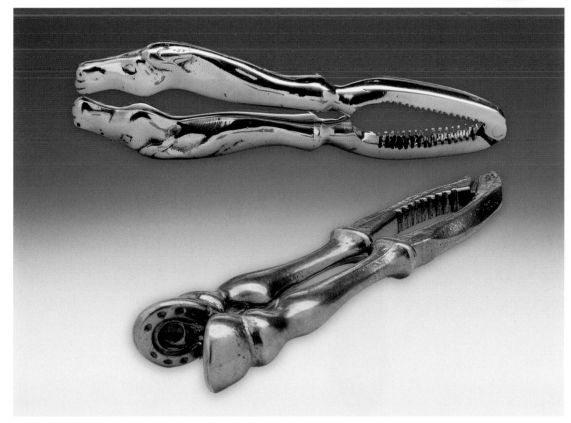

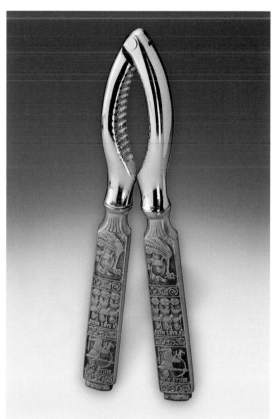

*Brass Levers (with Equestrian Theme)*
[top] 20th Century, Argentina
[bottom] 1910, England
Brass; [longest] 6.25" (16 cm)

*Engraved Lever (with Norwegian Historical Scenes)*
Middle 20th Century, Norway
Chrome/Pewter (handles); 6.25" (16 cm)

*Different Designs and Miscellaneous Metals*
[top] 1906, United States, 6.75" (14.5 cm); [center-left] 19th Century, France, 7" (18 cm);
[center-right] Early 20th Century, France, 5.25" (13.5 cm); [bottom-left] 1927, United States, 5" (12.5 cm);
[bottom-right] 1879, United States, 5.5" (14 cm)
*(The center-right piece is aluminum, and the bottom-right piece is painted iron.)*

*Plier with Spring*
19th Century, Germany
Silver Plate/Brass; 6.5" (16.5 cm)

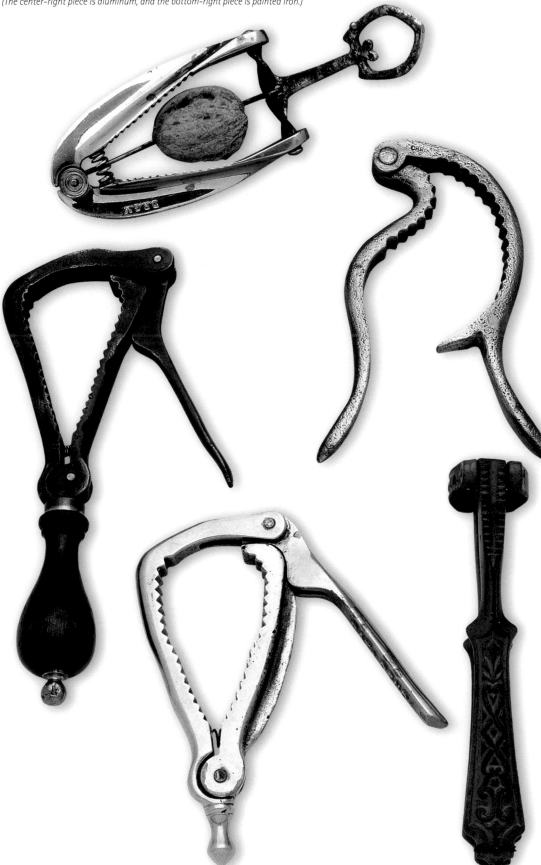

*Small Pocket Lever*
19th Century, England
Brass; 3" (7.5 cm)

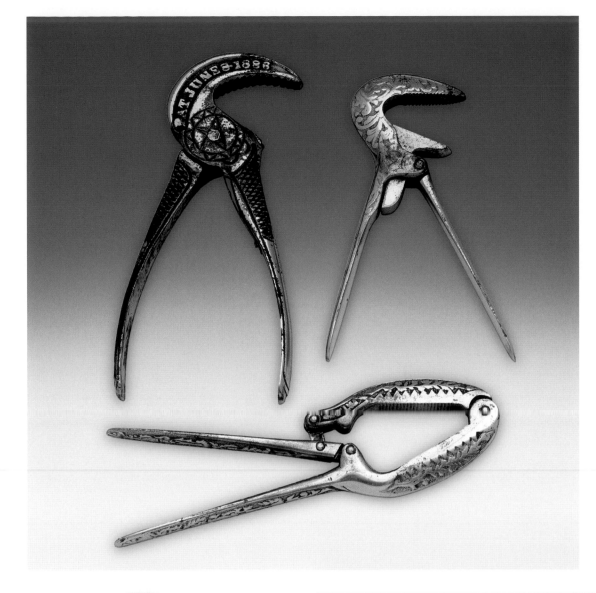

*Early American Lever Designs*
United States
[left] 1886, 6.5" (16.5 cm); [right] 1892, 6" (15.5 cm);
[front] 1890, 6.75" (17 cm)
Iron

*Early American Lever Designs (detail)*
Note the star-shaped embellishment stamped into this
iron nutcracker patented in 1886.

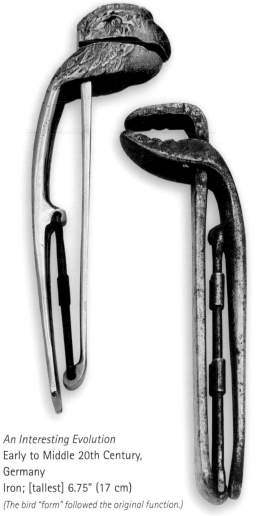

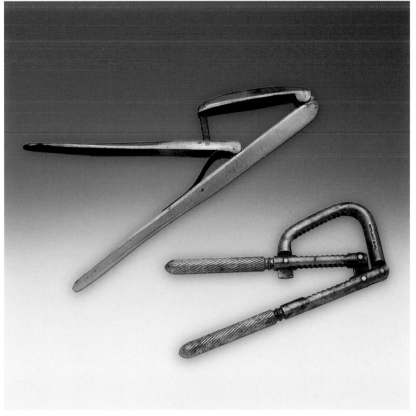

*An Interesting Evolution*
Early to Middle 20th Century,
Germany
Iron; [tallest] 6.75" (17 cm)
*(The bird "form" followed the original function.)*

*Early American Levers*
United States
[top] 1878, 8" (20.5 cm); [bottom] 1894, 5.5" (14 cm)
Steel

*Interesting Reversible Levers*
19th Century, Europe
Iron; [largest] 6" (15 cm)

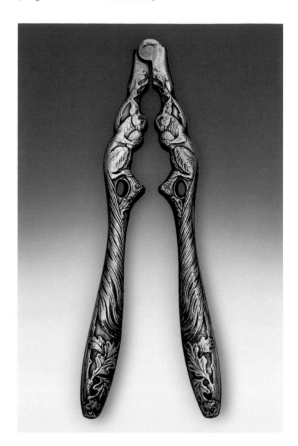

*Lever Decorated with Rabbits*
Early 20th Century, Germany
Silver Plate/Iron; 6.5" (16.5 cm)
*(designed to crack two sizes of nuts)*

*Unique Nutcracker (with Squirrel Figure)*
Early 20th Century, Germany
Iron; 9" (23 cm)

*Vulture Head*
Middle 20th Century, Germany
Brass/Enamel; 6.75" (17 cm)

*Maritime Design (Featuring Ship and Anchor)*
1900, England
Iron; 6.25" (16 cm)

*Ape and Dragon Heads*
[left] 1875, England, 7" (18 cm);
[right] 1850, France, 6.75" (17 cm);
Iron

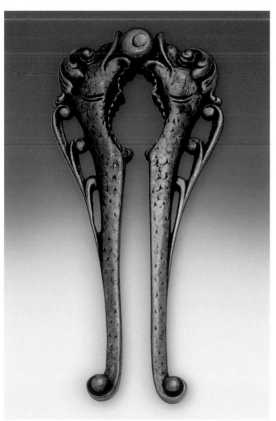

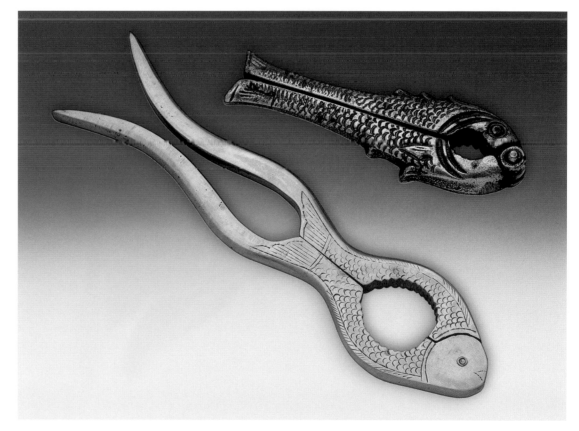

*Dolphins*
Early 19th Century, France
Bronze; 6.5" (16.5 cm)

*A Small School of Fish*
20th Century
[top] England; Burnished Cast Iron; 5" (12.5 cm)
[bottom] Israel; Brass; 8.5" (21.5 cm)

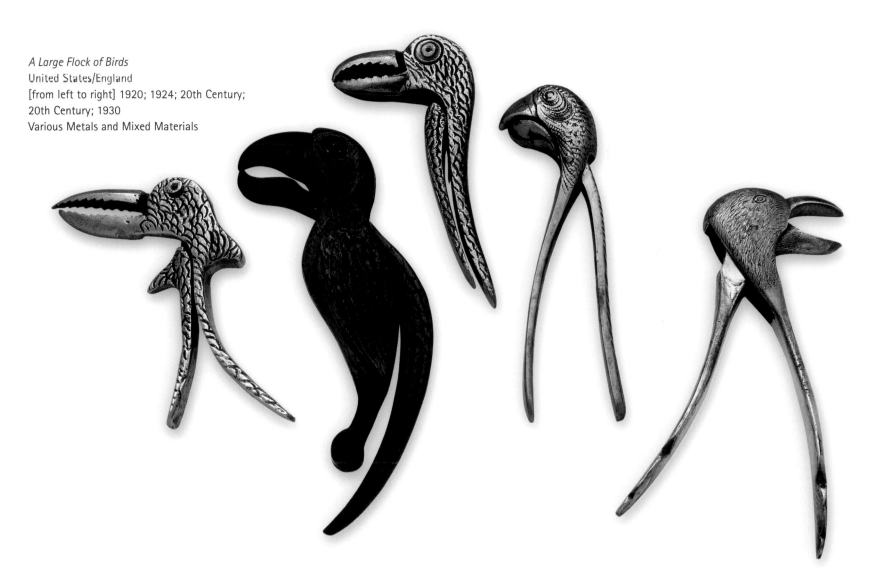

*A Large Flock of Birds*
United States/England
[from left to right] 1920; 1924; 20th Century;
20th Century; 1930
Various Metals and Mixed Materials

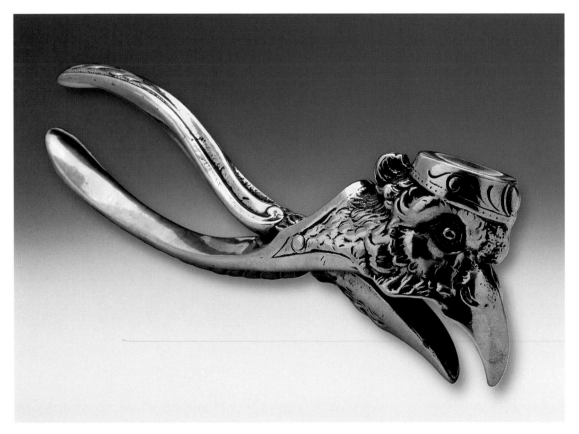

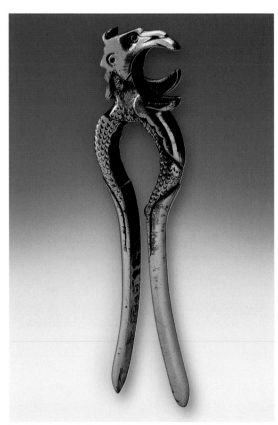

*Eagle with Crown*
Middle 19th Century, England
Brass; 7" (18 cm)

*Griffin*
1880, France
Iron; 6.25" (16 cm)

*Ape Head with Glass Eyes*
1900, France
Silver Plate/Iron; 6" (15.5 cm)

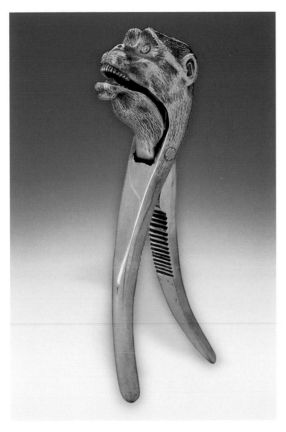

*Monkeys*
Early 19th Century, England
Iron/Copper Wash; 5.75" (14.5 cm)

*A Pack of Interesting Animals*
England
[top-left] Bronze, 3.5" (9 cm); [bottom-left] Brass, 1928, 2.75" (7 cm);
[center] Brass, 1930, 5.5" (14 cm); [far-right] Brass, 1930, 5.25" (13.5 cm)

*Pelican*
Middle 20th Century, Israel
Brass/Enamel; 5.25" (13.5 cm)

*Best in Show: A Collection of Dog Figures*
[clockwise from front-left]
19th Century, United States; Iron/Enamel; 3.75" (9.5 cm);
19th Century, United States; Iron; 6.25" (16 cm);
20th Century, Argentina; Copper Plate; 6.25" (16 cm);
1910, Germany; Iron (Chrome Base); 5.75" (14.5 cm);
Early 20th Century, England; Bronze; 5.75" (14.5 cm)

*(This particular nutcracker is also a tobacco cutter—note the blade under the chest.)*

*Large Dog (on Ornate Base)*
Early 20th Century, France
Bronze; 9.75" (25 cm)

*Hunting Dog in Pointer Position*
Late 20th Century, United States
Iron; 8" (20.5 cm)

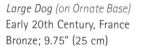

A Group of Uncommon Squirrel Nutcrackers
[clockwise from front-left]
1900, United States; Iron; 6.5" (16.5 cm);
Early 20th Century, United States; Copper Plate; 8.75" (22 cm);
20th Century, Germany; Bronze; 6.5" (16.5 cm);
Early 20th Century, United States; Copper Plate; 5.75" (14.5 cm)

Squirrels
[left] Early 20th Century, Germany; [right] 1878, United States
Iron; [largest] 9" (23 cm)

Kangaroo
1930, England
Iron; 5.5" (14 cm)

Marketing Piece for Ariel Motorcycle Company
Early 20th Century, England
Iron; 7" (18 cm)
(Note the "A" on the horse's nose.)

*Ibex*
20th Century, Russia
Copper Alloy; 9.5" (24 cm)

*Lions (detail)*
The tail of this lion serves as the handle for opening the mouth, where strong, jagged teeth securely hold the nut in place.

*Hippopotamus Head*
Early 20th Century, England
Iron; [height] 3.25" (8 cm)

*Lions*
[front] 19th Century, United States; Iron; 7" (18 cm);
[back] 20th Century, England; Bronze; 6" (15 cm)

*Dragons*
Russia
[front] Early 20th Century; Iron
[back] Middle 20th Century; Copper Alloy
[tallest] 3.5" (9 cm)

*An Imposing Dinosaur*
1920, England
Iron; 5.25" (13.5 cm)

*Fish with Glass Eyes*
1930, England
Nickel Plate/Iron; 3.75" (9.5 cm)

*Crocodiles*
19th/20th Century, United States/England
Iron/Brass/Bronze; [longest] 15.75" (40 cm);
[shortest] 7.5" (19 cm)
*(The figure at the far-right has copper plating.)*

111

*Eagle with Crown*
1880, Germany
Bronze; 5.75" (14.5 cm)

*Various Animal Castings*
United States
[bear] Late 20th Century, 5.5" (14 cm); [animal head] 1920, 4.75" (12 cm);
[elephant] Early 20th Century, 4.75" (12 cm);
Iron

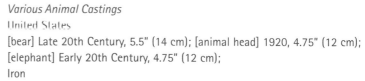

*Fish Tabletop Nutcracker*
1850, England
Brass; 2.75" (7 cm)

*Decorative Lever Nutcrackers*
20th Century, Israel
Brass/Enamel; [height, from front to back]
2" (5 cm); 3" (7.5 cm); 2.75" (7 cm)

*Birds*
United States
[from front to back] 1860, 6.75" (17 cm);
Early 20th Century, 4.5" (11.5 cm);
Early 20th Century, 5.75" (14.5 cm)
Iron

*Attractive, Modern Nutcrackers*
Late 20th Century
[fish] Aluminum, United States
[other animals] Chrome Plate/Iron, Asia
[largest] 6.25" (16 cm)

*Frog*
1900, France
Silver Plating/Brass; 5" (12.5 cm)

*Souvenir Nutcrackers*
20th Century, United States
Brass; [largest] 5.25" (13.5 cm)

*Two-Sided Levers*
Late 19th/Early 20th Century, England
Brass; 5" (12.5 cm)

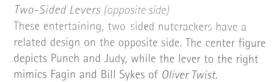

*Two-Sided Levers (opposite side)*
These entertaining, two-sided nutcrackers have a related design on the opposite side. The center figure depicts Punch and Judy, while the lever to the right mimics Fagin and Bill Sykes of *Oliver Twist*.

*Various Fowl (detail)*
An interesting chased detail encircles the hinge mechanism and outlines the bird.

*Various Fowl*
[from left to right] Late 19th Century, England; Brass; 5.75" (14.5 cm);
Late 19th Century, England; Brass; 6.75" (17 cm);
Early 20th Century, United States; Brass/Bronze; 7.75" (19.5 cm);
1900, Russia; Bronze; 6.25" (16 cm)

*Large Lever (Featuring Human Face)*
1800, England
Bronze; 8.25" (21 cm)

*Various Lever Designs*
Late 19th/Early 20th Century, England
Brass; [largest] 7" (18 cm); [smallest] 4.5" (11.5 cm)

*Lion, Dog, and Clown*
Late 19th Century, England
Brass; [tallest] 7.25" (18.5 cm)

*Ship, Mermaid, and Nymph*
1880, England
Brass; [tallest] 2.5" (6.5 cm)

*Humpty Dumpty*
Late 19th Century, England
Bronze; 5.75" (14.5 cm)

*A Loving Couple*
Early 20th Century, India
Silver Plate/Brass; 6" (15 cm)

*Souvenir Nutcrackers*
20th Century, England
Brass; [largest] 3" (7.5 cm)

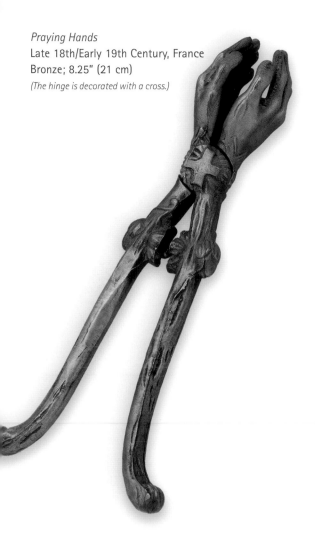

*Praying Hands*
Late 18th/Early 19th Century, France
Bronze; 8.25" (21 cm)
*(The hinge is decorated with a cross.)*

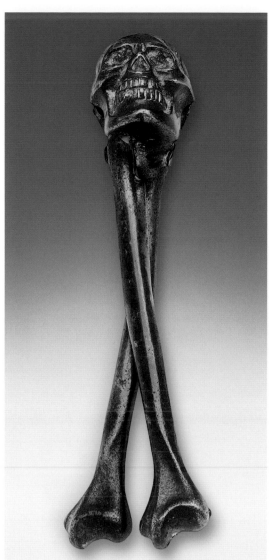

*Skull and Crossbones*
1928, England
Iron; 6" (15.5 cm)

*Skull and Crossbones (detail)*
This nutcracker utilizes the haunting subject matter found on the flag of a pirate ship.

*An Elegant Pair of Hands*
Early 20th Century, France
Silver Plate/Brass; 4.25" (11 cm)

*Clown*
1930, Germany
Iron; 5.75" (14.5 cm)

*Rare African American Casting*
Late 19th Century, United States
Iron; 7.75" (19.5 cm)

*Otto von Bismarck*
Late 19th/Early 20th Century, Germany
Bronze; 7.5" (19 cm)

*Otto von Bismarck (detail)*
Amazing engravings grace the handles of this wonderful nutcracker, which represents Germany's first chancellor.

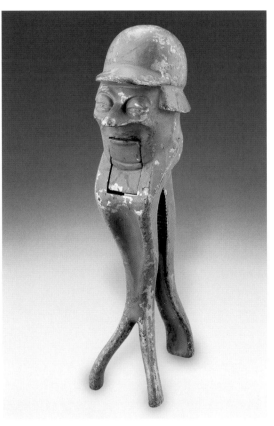

*WWI Soldier*
1930, United States
Aluminum; 8" (20.5 cm)

*A Jolly Gnome*
Late 19th Century, Origin Unknown
Brass; 9.5" (24 cm)

118

*Sailor (Self-Standing)*
1900, France
Silver; 5" (12.5 cm)

*Imaginative Gentlemen Nutcrackers (Self-Standing)*
Late 19th/Early 20th Century, England
Brass; [tallest] 6" (15.5 cm)

*Buccaneer Bust*
19th Century, France
Bronze; 4.25" (11 cm)

*Expressive Male Figure*
19th Century, England
Brass; 8.5" (21.5 cm)
*(American collectors affectionately refer to this figure as "Mr. Magoo.")*

Adam and Eve
1880, England
Iron; 7.75" (19.5 cm)

*Adam and Eve (detail)*
A spectacular rendering of the famous biblical characters Adam and Eve, complete with serpent and forbidden fruit.

*Neptune (God of the Sea)*
Late 19th Century, France
Brass; 8.25" (21 cm)
*(Small nuts crack under his toes; large nuts crack beneath his seat.)*

*Kissing Couples*
Middle 20th Century, United States
Brass; 6.25" (16 cm)

*Two French Soldiers*
Late 19th Century, France
Bronze; 6.5" (16.5 cm)
*(Nuts are cracked inside the helmet.)*

*Brave Hunter and Forest Spirit*
Early 20th Century, Russia
Copper Alloy; [height] 6.5" (16.5 cm)

*Lovely French Nude*
1900, France
Silver Plate/Brass; 3.5" (9 cm)

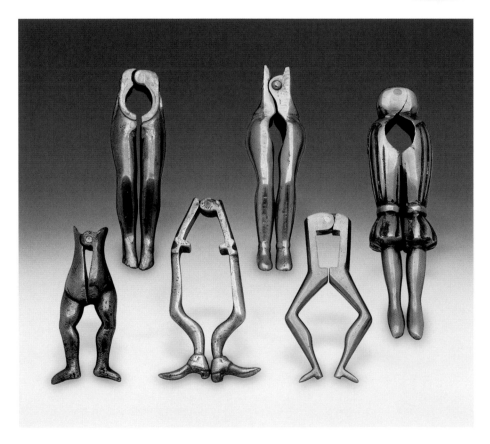

*Shapely Victorian Legs*
Middle 19th/Early 20th Century, England/France/United States
Brass, [largest] 6" (15.5 cm); [smallest] 3.5" (9 cm)

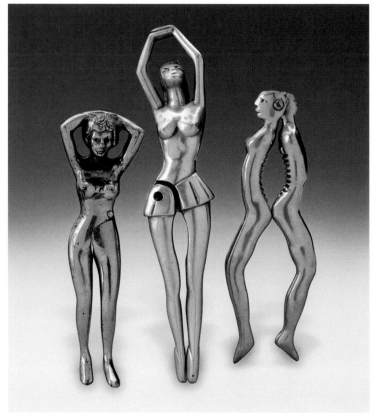

*Female Figures*
[from left to right] 1930, England; Silver Plate/Brass; 6.25" (16 cm);
20th Century, United States; Aluminum; 7.75" (20 cm);
20th Century, United States; Aluminum; 6.25" (16 cm)

*French Courtesan*
1890, France
Brass; 8.5" (21.5 cm)

*Walnut-Shaped Nutcracker*
Early 20th Century, Germany
Brass; 3.25" (8 cm)

*French Courtesan (detail)*
A stunning sculpture with amazing detail of face, hair, and costume. The torso lifts off and reveals the cracking device

*Sailor, Asian Caricature, and Birds*
*Sailor, Asian Caricature, and Birds*
Late 19th Century, United States
Iron; [clockwise from top-left] 7.75" (19.5 cm);
6.25" (16 cm); 6.25" (16 cm); 7" (18 cm)

*Unusual Table Nutcracker (for Large and Small Nuts)*
Late 18th/Early 19th Century, France
Brass; [height] 1.5" (4 cm)

*Decorative Table Nutcracker*
19th Century, Germany
Iron; [height] 2.5" (6.5 cm)

*Standing Cast Iron Characters*
1870, United States
Iron; [left] 11.25" (28.5 cm); [right] 11" (28 cm)

graceful

# metal screw nutcrackers

Like the wood screw nutcracker, the metal screw did not make an appearance until the 17th century. Most of the earliest of these were made of iron, but some were made of brass and silver. Usually these were small in size and meant to be carried in the pocket. While most were simple in design, the brass and silver were more malleable and allowed for more intricate detail.

*The metal screw followed the metal lever by several centuries.*

In 1871, the H. M. Quackenbush Company of New York produced a cast iron screw nutcracker that has been reproduced by the thousands over the years. Today you will find it nickel plated in many local grocery and kitchen shops.

*Elegant Silver Screw*
18th Century, France
Silver; 2.5" (6.5 cm)

*Pocket Screws*
17th/18th Century, England/France
Brass/Iron; [largest] 3.25" (8 cm)

*Pocket Screw Pair*
1733, Holland
Brass; 2" (5 cm);
*(One screw features the date 1733; the other has a wax seal stamp.)*

*Simple Pocket Screws*
18th Century, England
Brass/Iron; [largest] 2.5" (6.5 cm)

*Classic Pocket Screw*
18th Century, England
Bronze; 4.25" (11 cm)

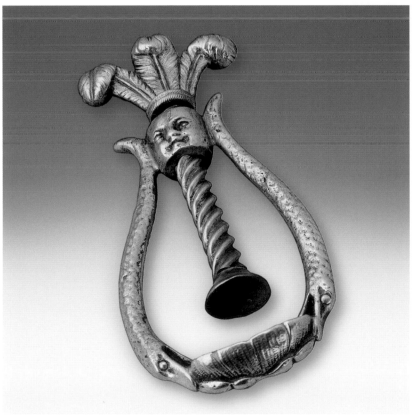

*Decorative Screw with Face and Plume*
18th Century, France
Brass; 3.75" (9.5 cm)

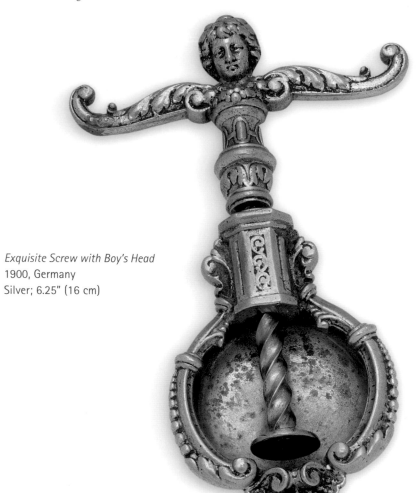

*Exquisite Screw with Boy's Head*
1900, Germany
Silver; 6.25" (16 cm)

*Exquisite Screw with Boy's Head (detail)*
This nutcracker of exceptional beauty and charm features amazing detail of face, ornate handles, and decoration.

*Decorative Screw*
Late 19th Century, France
Silver; 3.5" (9 cm)

*Delightful Girl in Hoop Skirt*
Middle 20th Century, England
Brass; 4" (10 cm)

Long-Handled Screws
19th Century, France
Mixed Materials; [tallest] 9.5" (24 cm)

Table Screws
[left]19th Century, England; [right] Middle 20th Century, Germany
Silver Plate; [largest] 4" (10 cm)
*(The screw shown to the left utilizes ivory standards; the right-hand screw displays zodiac symbols.)*

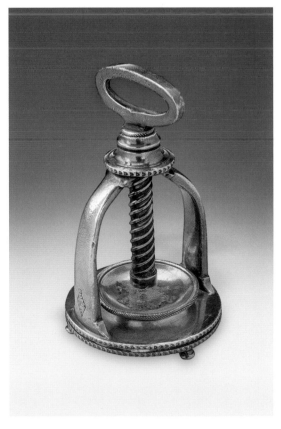

A Grouping of Table Screws
19th/20th Century, Germany
Iron; [largest] 4.75" (12 cm)

Table Screw
19th Century, France
Silver; 3.25" (8.5 cm)

*Various Shapes and Styles of Screws*
19th/20th Centuries, Europe
Brass; [tallest] 6.25" (16 cm);
[shortest] 3.25" (8.5 cm)

*Dated Ring Screw*
1841, England
Silver Plate; 3.5" (9 cm)

*Walnut Table Screw*
1910, France
Silver; 4.5" (11.5 cm)
*(by Christophe)*

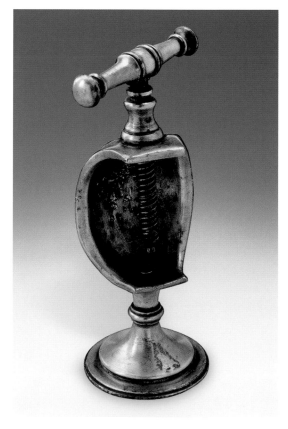

*Walnut Table Screw (detail)*
This beautiful nutcracker has the surface detail of
a true walnut shell and a cavity large enough to crack
this delicious nut.

Handsome Male Figure
19th Century, France
Bronze; 8" (20.5 cm)

Table Screw
Early 20th Century, Germany
Silver Plate; 5.5" (14 cm)

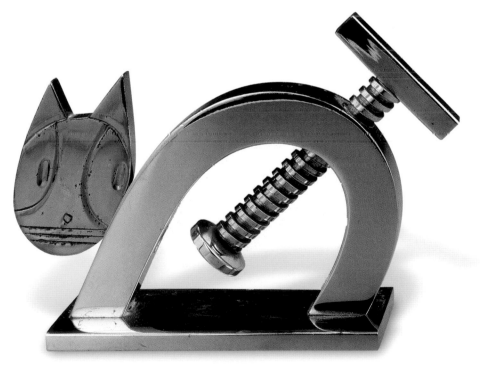

Stylized Cat Screw
Early 20th Century, Austria
Chrome; [height] 3" (7.5 cm)

Quackenbush Nutcracker
20th Century, United States
Chrome Plate; 5" (12.5 cm)
(This design was first patented in 1871.)

*A Collection of Screw Nutcrackers*
Early 20th Century, Germany/United States
Chrome Plate/Stainless Steel;
[largest] 5.75" (14.5 cm); [smallest] 2.75" (7 cm)

In the past, metal was an expensive commodity. Often, especially in times of war, items were melted down for use in a new product. We wonder what beautiful nut-crackers, considered luxury items, may have been lost in this manner.

*Brazil Nut, Walnut, and Squirrel (detail)*
Traditional German workmanship makes this screw strong enough to crack the hardest of nuts.

*Brazil Nut, Walnut, and Squirrel*
20th Century, Germany
Bronze; 3.25" (8.5 cm)

tough

# metal percussion nutcrackers

The hammer has been the most common of all percussion tools used in civilized times to crack open the hard shell of a nut. Special hammers were designed just for this purpose. To complement the nut hammer, the "knee warmer" was invented around 1850.

> *The hammer has been the most common of all percussion tools.*

This consisted of a curved square or round piece of iron that fit over the leg just above the knee. A raised pedestal in the center held the nut to be cracked. The force of the hammer when cracking the nut did not hurt the leg, as the pressure was spread over a greater area. A different cast iron hammer was invented in the late 19th century. This type of nutcracker operated by lifting a heavy hammer and letting it drop on the nut. Nut bowls with hammers or other percussion nutcrackers can still be found in many homes today.

*Heavy Cast Iron Figure*
Late 19th Century, United States
Iron; 9" (23 cm)

*Knee Warmers and Hammer*
1850, United States
Iron; [hammer] 6.75" (17 cm);
[warmers–from left to right] 3" (7.5 cm);
2.25" (5.5 cm)

*Bowls with Metal Plungers*
Early 20th Century, United States
Bronze/Iron; [front] 9.5" (24 cm); [back] 7" (18 cm)

*Bowl and Hammer Set*
Early 20th Century, United States
Bronze/Iron/Wood Bowl; [bowl—height] 3.25" (8.5 cm);
[hammer—length] 9" (23 cm)

Registered in 1897, the English "Tough Nut" is one of the most sought-after collectibles today. The nut is inserted in the hollow of the chest, and the man is hit on the head to crack the nut.

*Tough Nut (detail)*
The Tough Nut depicts a smiling sailor sitting on a lobster pot. This is one of the first metal, figural percussion nutcrackers.

*Tough Nut*
1897, England
Iron; 7.75" (19.5 cm)

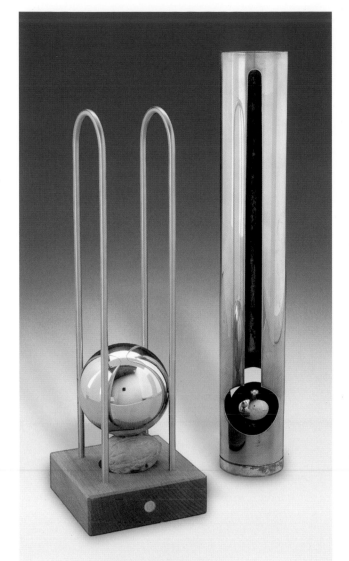

*Ball Percussion Nutcrackers*
1994, Sweden/Germany
Silver Plate; [tallest] 14" (35 cm)

*Hammer with Walnut Pedestal*
Early 20th Century, United States
Silver Plate; [hammer—length] 6.5" (16.5 cm);
[pedestal—height] 2.75" (7 cm)

*Hammer Nutcracker*
Late 19th Century, United States
Iron; [height] 3" (7.5 cm)

ingenious

# metal mechanical nutcrackers

Since the American Patent Office opened in 1836, hundreds of mechanical nutcrackers have been patented in the United States. One of the first was the Blake nutcracker, patented in 1853. This nutcracker was strong enough to crack even the obstinate shell of the black walnut that was native to America.

*As commercial production of nuts grew, so did the size and speed of nutcrackers.*

Other nutcrackers soon followed, and American ingenuity was truly at its best in the many ways the hard nut shell was cracked. One invention was not only a nutcracker, but a tobacco cutter and cork press as well.

For pecan growers, a nutcracker that would put pressure on the shell from both ends was needed. Cracking the nut in this way would help achieve the unbroken halves that were so much in demand by candy makers and bakers, as well as consumers. Many clamp-on table nutcrackers were made especially for pecans in the early 20th century.

As commercial production of nuts grew, so did the size and speed of nutcrackers. Today nuts glide on conveyor belts to cracking machines that can crack over 800 nuts every minute.

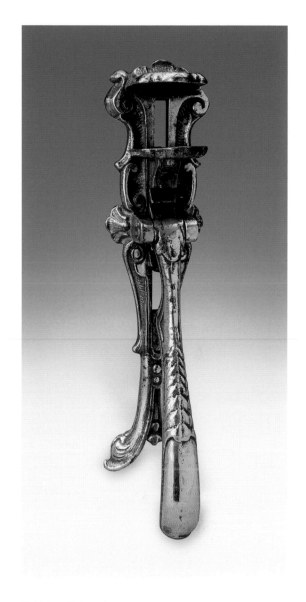

*Tabletop Nutcracker*
Early 20th Century, Germany
Steel/Chrome Plate; 11" (28 cm)

*Heavy Lever Nutcracker*
Late 19th Century, United States
Iron; 9" (23 cm)

The United States produces eighty percent
of the world's supply of pecans and thirty-eight
percent of all walnuts—but only about three
percent of hazelnuts.

*Various Mechanical Nutcrackers*
Late 19th/Early 20th Century, United States
Iron; [tallest] 5" (13 cm)

*Bowl with Screw*
Patented 1923, United States
Brass; 9" (23 cm)

*Blake Nutcrackers with Variations*
United States
[from left to right] 1856; 1856; 1853
Iron; [largest] 6" (15.5 cm)
*(The right-hand nutcracker is an original Blake from 1853; the other two are based on this initial design.)*

*The Little Giant*
Patented 1881, United States
Iron; 9.5" (24 cm)

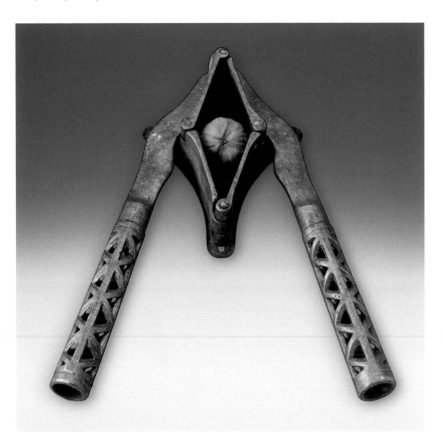

*Pecan Clamp Nutcrackers*
Early 20th Century, United States
Iron; [largest] 10.25" (26 cm);
[smallest] 8.25" (21 cm)

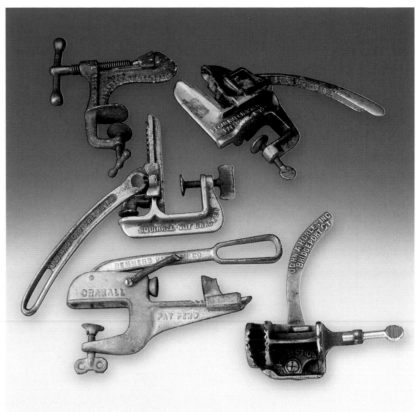

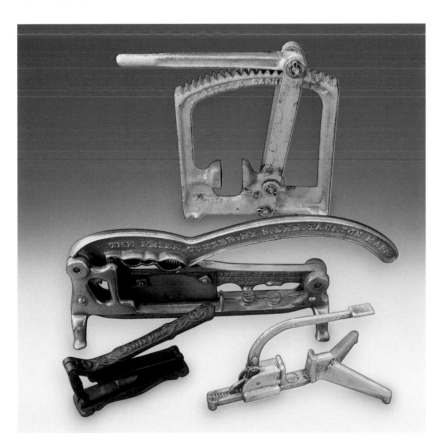

*Mechanical Table Nutcrackers*
Early 20th Century, Germany/United States
Iron; [tallest] 11.75" (30 cm)

*(Front-left nutcracker is by Knirps; rear nutcracker is by Potter.)*

*Large Pecan Clamp Nutcracker*
1912, United States
Iron; 10.5" (26.5 cm)

intriguing

142

# betel cutters

Although not truly nutcrackers, betel cutters are often included in nutcracker collections. Betel cutters have existed in the Asian societies of India and neighboring countries since 1500 A.D. The design of betel cutters differs from area to area, but traditionally the cutting blade is iron.

> *Betel cutters are often included in nutcracker collections.*

Today many early cutters are duplicated entirely in brass for the growing tourist market. This hinged instrument is used to slice the areca nut (or *supari*, the Indian name), which is then wrapped in a betel leaf along with lime from seashells. Other ingredients such as tobacco or spices may be added. The quid is then placed in the mouth between the gum and cheek and is left there for hours. The large amount of red saliva produced by the betel quid discolors the user's lips, gums, and teeth. If not cleaned regularly, teeth will eventually become black. Dentists have been known to make false teeth of ebony so as to match the surrounding teeth.

Throughout history, betel chewing has played a major role in many facets of life such as entertaining, marriage, and the etiquette of the courts. The medicinal qualities of the addictive areca nut are questionable, but it gives a feeling of euphoria and therefore is used by many to ease anxiety or pain.

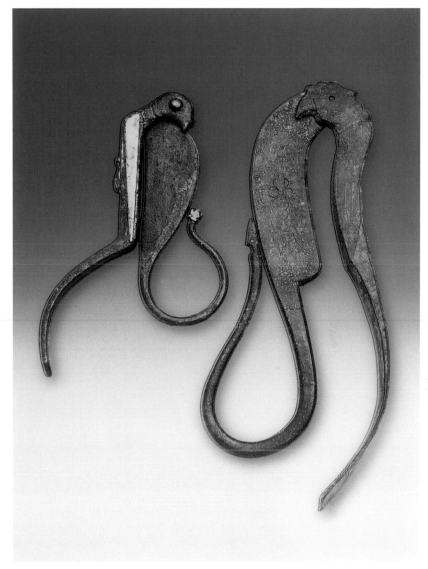

*Rare Chinese Betel Cutters*
18th Century, China
Iron; [largest] 6.5" (16.5 cm)

*Lady with Praying Hands*
19th Century, Sri Lanka
Brass/Iron Blade; 8.25" (21 cm)

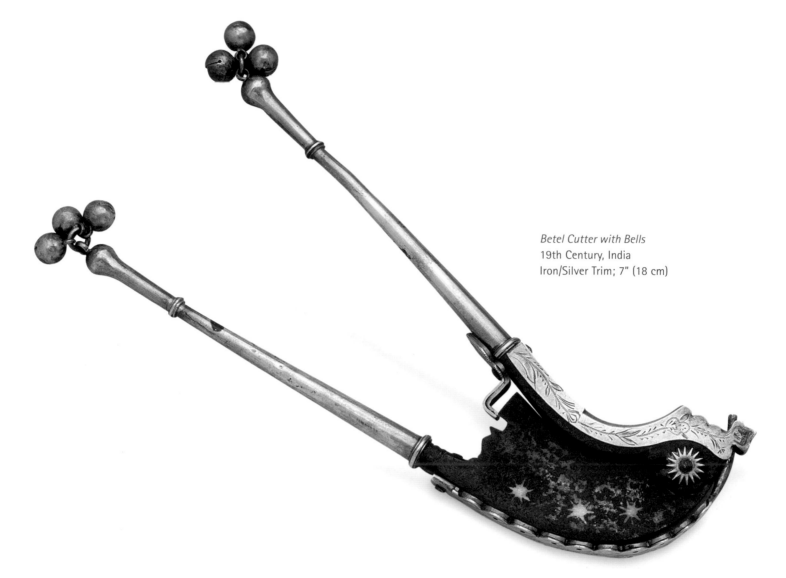

*Betel Cutter with Bells*
19th Century, India
Iron/Silver Trim; 7" (18 cm)

*Betel Cutters with Silver Inlay*
19th Century, Burma
Iron/Silver Trim; 5" (12.5 cm)

*Betel Cutters with Silver and Gold Inlay*
19th Century, India
Iron/Silver and Gold Trim; [front] 6.25" (16 cm); [top left] 5" (12.5 cm);
[top right] 4.25" (11 cm)

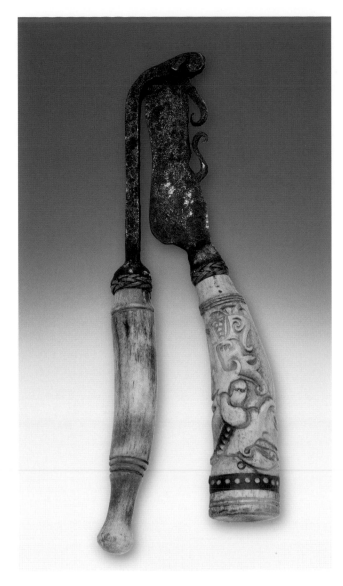

*Betel Cutter with Engraved Bone Handle*
17th Century, India
Iron/Bone; 6.5" (16.5 cm)

*Unusual Betel Cutters*
18th Century, Ceylon/Borneo/Indonesia
Iron/Silver Trim; [from top to bottom] 5.5" (14 cm); 8" (20.5 cm); 8.5" (21.5 cm)

*Horse*
19th Century, India
Brass/Iron Blade; 5" (12.5 cm)

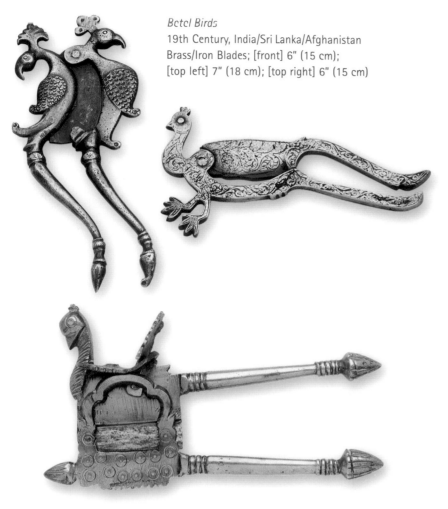

*Betel Birds*
19th Century, India/Sri Lanka/Afghanistan
Brass/Iron Blades; [front] 6" (15 cm);
[top left] 7" (18 cm); [top right] 6" (15 cm)

*Double-Bladed Betel Cutters*
19th Century, India
Brass; [largest] 7.5" (19 cm)

*Ornate Betel Cutter (detail)*
Numerous insets of turquoise originally decorated
this extraordinary betel cutter. In addition, ivory covers
each handle and small mirrors complete the unique
decoration.

*Ornate Betel Cutter*
1850, Kashmir
Iron/Ivory Trim; 8" (20.5 cm)

*Figural Betel Cutters*
19th Century, India
Brass/Iron Blades; [largest] 6.75" (17 cm)

*Figural Betel Cutters* (detail)
Over the years, many romantic themes have been
incorporated in the design of betel cutters.

According to a well-respected
encyclopedia, at one time
the practice of chewing betel
affected nearly one-tenth of
the world's population. Today,
young people are turning
away from this habit, especially
in more industrialized areas.

*Young Lovers*
19th Century, India
Silver/Iron Blade; 4.25" (11 cm)

*A Royal Cutter* (Featuring Eagle Design)
1820, India
Silver/Iron Blade; 6.25" (16 cm)
*(This betel cutter formerly belonged to the Maharajah of Jodhpur.)*

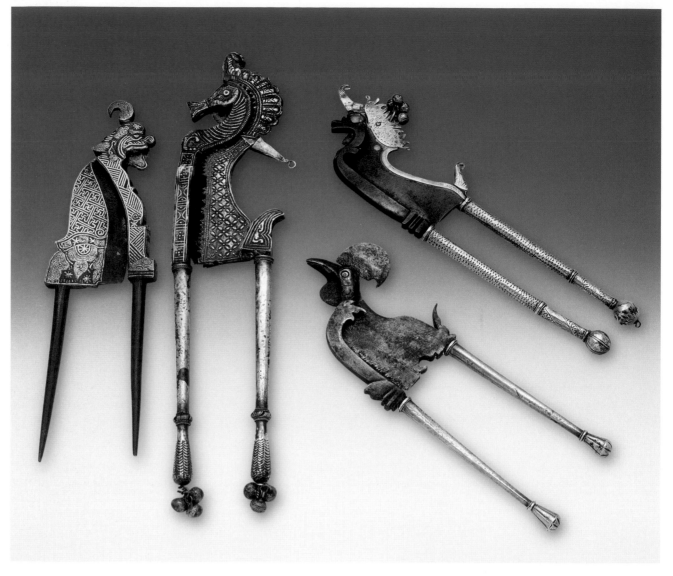

*Betel Cutters (with Silver Sleeves)*
19th Century, Indonesia
Iron/Silver
[left] 8.75" (22 cm);
[middle] 11" (28 cm);
[bottom-right] 7.75" (19.5 cm);
[top-right] 9" (23 cm)

*Various Betel Cutters*
19th Century, India
Brass/Iron Blades
[largest] 7.25" (18.5 cm);
[smallest] 5" (12.5 cm)

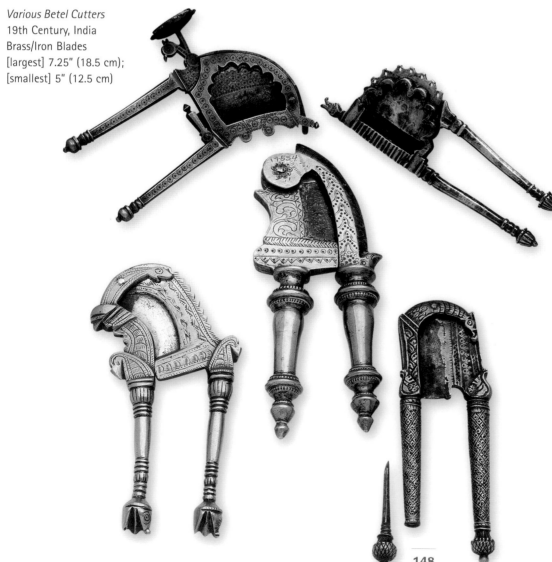

*Various Betel Cutters (detail)*
A small steel cutting blade is hidden in one of this betel cutter's handles, and tiny pincers are contained inside the other.

148

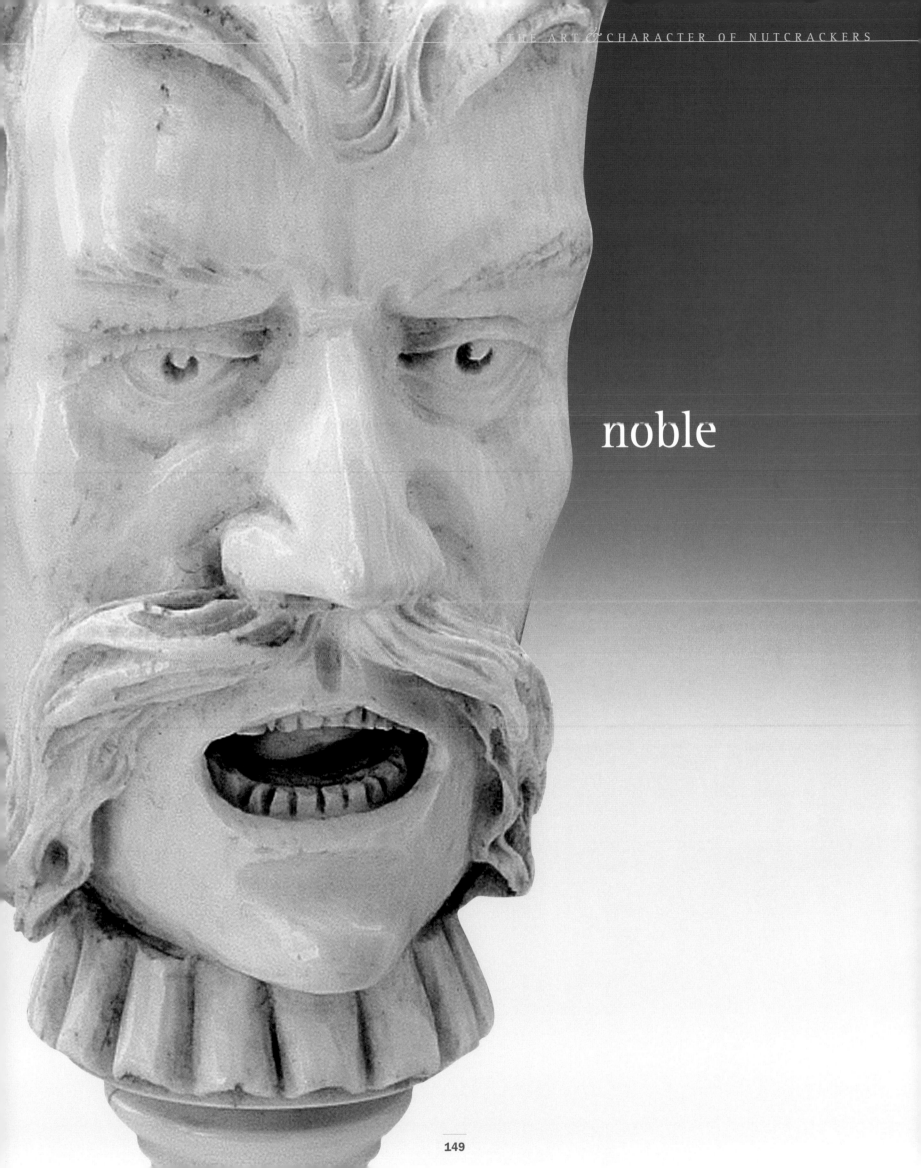

noble

# ivory and porcelain nutcrackers

Only a few nutcrackers made entirely of ivory exist today, most of which are from the 18th and 19th centuries. Although ivory is relatively easy to carve, it is not strong enough to endure the continued rigors of cracking hard-shelled nuts. Therefore, nearly every all-ivory nutcracker is of the screw type, where pressure to crack the nut is gradually increased. More common are nutcrackers trimmed with ivory, such as metal nutcrackers with ivory handles, or wooden nutcrackers with ivory insets.

> *Only a few nutcrackers made entirely of ivory exist today.*

Ivory darkens when exposed over time to bright light, and cracks easily when changes in humidity occur.

Porcelain nutcrackers were made in the late 19th and early 20th centuries and were meant to be used for cracking nuts at the dining table. The Meissen porcelain company near Dresden produced nutcrackers that can be identified by the famous crossed swords stamped on the bottom. Rauenstein porcelains were produced in Thuringia, and those marked RPM were produced in Bohemia.

Most porcelain nutcrackers have metal screw mechanisms, though some were designed with a lever of porcelain or metal.

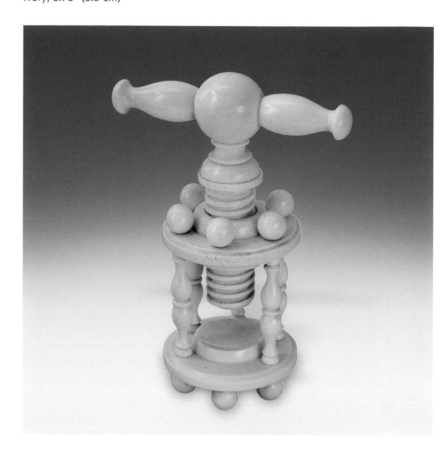

*Cage Screw*
Late 19th/Early 20th Century, Italy
Ivory; 3.75" (9.5 cm)

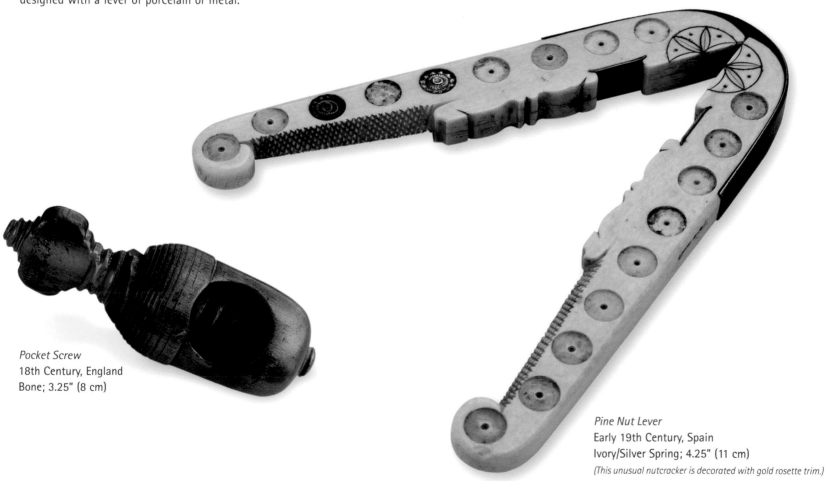

*Pocket Screw*
18th Century, England
Bone; 3.25" (8 cm)

*Pine Nut Lever*
Early 19th Century, Spain
Ivory/Silver Spring; 4.25" (11 cm)
*(This unusual nutcracker is decorated with gold rosette trim.)*

*Reversible Nutcracker with Silver Piqué*
19th Century, England
Ivory/Silver Plate; 6.25" (16 cm)

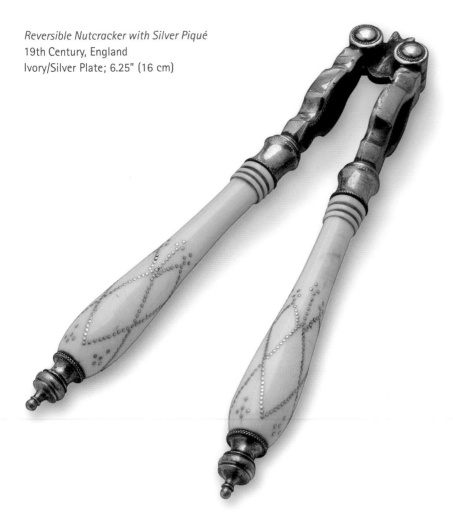

*Exceptional Screw with Iron Nail Trim*
Late 18th/Early 19th Century, France
Ivory/Iron; 3" (7.5 cm)

*Screws with Silver Trim*
Late 19th Century, England
Ivory/Silver; 3.25" (8 cm)

*A Pair of Hungry Squirrels*
[left] Late 19th Century, Switzerland
Wood; 7" (17.5 cm)
[right] Early 20th Century, France
Ivory; 6.5" (16.5 cm)

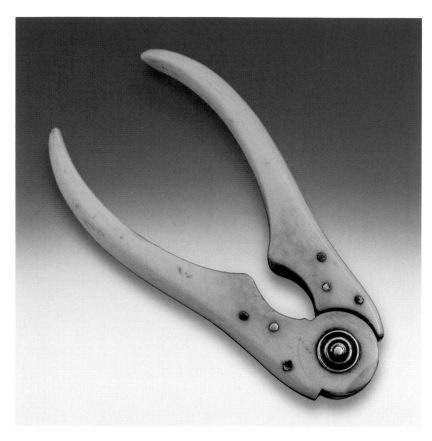

*Simple Ivory Lever*
19th Century, England
Ivory; 5" (12.5 cm)

*Talking Heads*
[left] Early 17th Century, France or Italy
[right] 17th Century, France
Ivory; [tallest] 6" (15.5 cm)

*Nutcrackers with Ivory Handles*
19th Century, England
Ivory/Silver Plate; [largest] 6.25" (16 cm)

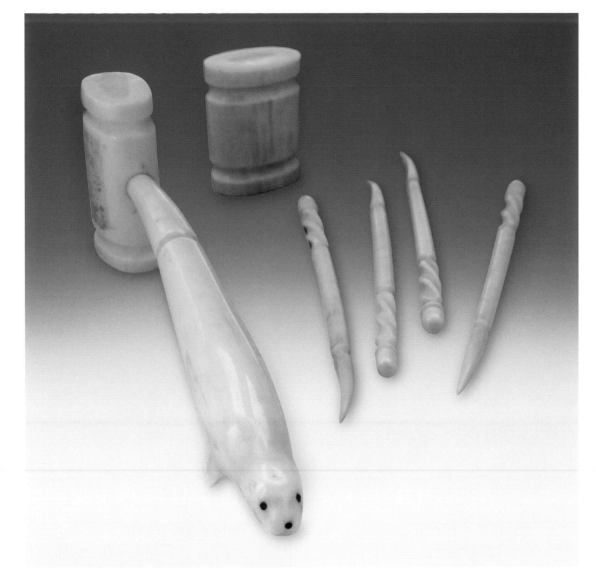

*Seal-Shaped Mallet, Pedestal, and Picks*
20th Century, United States (Alaska)
Walrus Tusk; [mallet] 7.25" (18.5 cm);
[pedestal] 2" (5 cm); [picks] 5.5" (14 cm)

*Seal-Shaped Mallet, Pedestal, and Picks (detail)*
A deep cavity carved into the pedestal holds the nut
firmly in place when being struck by the mallet. The ivory
picks were used to remove kernels from the shells.

*Ram*
19th Century, France
Ivory; 7.25" (18.5 cm)

*Ram (detail)*
A rich patina adds to the beauty of this exceptionally fine carving.
Note the elaborate monogram on the handle.

153

complementary

# nutcracker accessories

Many accessories were used in the cracking of nuts other than nutcrackers. Nut openers, pick-like instruments with a flattened end, have been used for centuries to open the walnut shell. During Victorian times, it was fashionable for both men and women to carry a fruit knife, and many of these held a nut pick. This accessory was generally made of sterling or recycled silver coins, as silver did not tarnish when cutting fruit.

Nutcrackers and nut picks became a part of the tableware and were created in the more popular silver service patterns. Special satin-lined boxes were made to store these items, and many sets included grape shears and fruit spoons.

Nut bowls were designed especially for unshelled nuts. Most were simple in design, crafted from wood or pottery. However, some bowls were beautifully molded in porcelain, glass, and silver.

> *Many accessories were used in the cracking of nuts.*

Sets of bowls were also created for shelled nuts. These sets consisted of a larger main bowl with a series of smaller matching dishes, into which the nuts were served with a special nut spoon. The nut spoon resembled a bonbon spoon, but with openwork in the bowl.

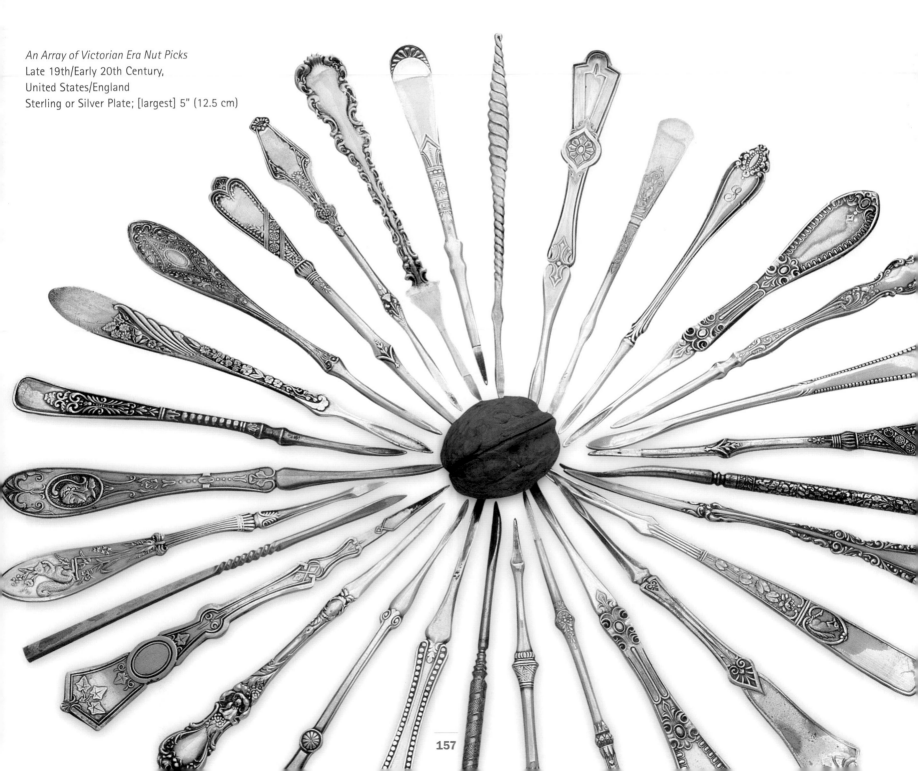

*An Array of Victorian Era Nut Picks*
Late 19th/Early 20th Century,
United States/England
Sterling or Silver Plate; [largest] 5" (12.5 cm)

*Victorian Nut Opener*
Late 19th/Early 20th Century, United States
Silver Plate/Brass; 7" (18 cm)

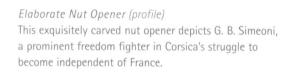

*Elaborate Nut Opener (profile)*
This exquisitely carved nut opener depicts G. B. Simeoni, a prominent freedom fighter in Corsica's struggle to become independent of France.

*Early Nut Opener*
14th Century, France
Iron; 5.25" (13.5 cm)

*Elaborate Nut Opener*
Late 18th Century, France (Corsica)
Walnut; 9" (23 cm)

*Pocket Fruit Knives (with Nut Picks)*
Late 19th/Early 20th Century, England/United States
Silver or Silver Plate; [largest] 3.5" (9 cm)

*Unusual Nut Opener*
Late 19th/Early 20th Century
Silver Plate; 5.75" (14.5 cm)

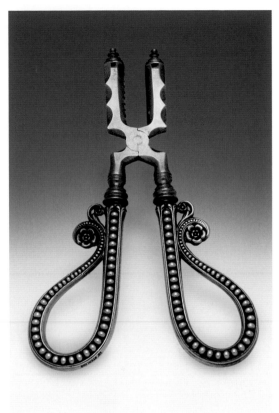

*Special Nut Spoons*
Late 19th/Early 20th Century
Sterling Silver; [from left to right] 5" (12.5 cm);
4.5" (11.5 cm); 5.25" (13.5 cm)

*Nut Bowls (for Whole Nuts)*
Early 20th Century, Japan
Porcelain; [tallest] 4.75" (12 cm)

*Nut Bowls (inner view)*
Lovely Japanese nut bowls such as these feature
meticulously painted nut designs, and often display
nuts in relief.

*Nut Bowl with Serving Dish*
Late 19th/Early 20th Century, Japan
Porcelain/Gold Trim; [bowl height] 2.25" (5.5 cm);
[dish height] 1.25" (3 cm)

*Nut Bowl and Cup*
Early 20th Century, Japan
Porcelain; [bowl height] 3" (7.5 cm);
[cup height] 1.5" (4 cm)

*Nut Bowl and Cup (inner view)*
The interior of this wonderful Japanese nut bowl is
adorned with a beautiful nut-and-leaf design.

*Delicate Glass Nut Bowl*
Late 19th/Early 20th Century, United States
Glass/Silver Plate; 9" (23 cm)

*Sterling Silver Nut Bowl*
1900, United States
Sterling Silver; 9.25" (23.5 cm)

*Pedestal Nut Bowl*
19th Century, United States
Silver Plate; 9" (23 cm)

*Nut Bowl with Squirrel-Shaped Handles*
19th Century, United States
Silver Plate; 6" (15 cm)

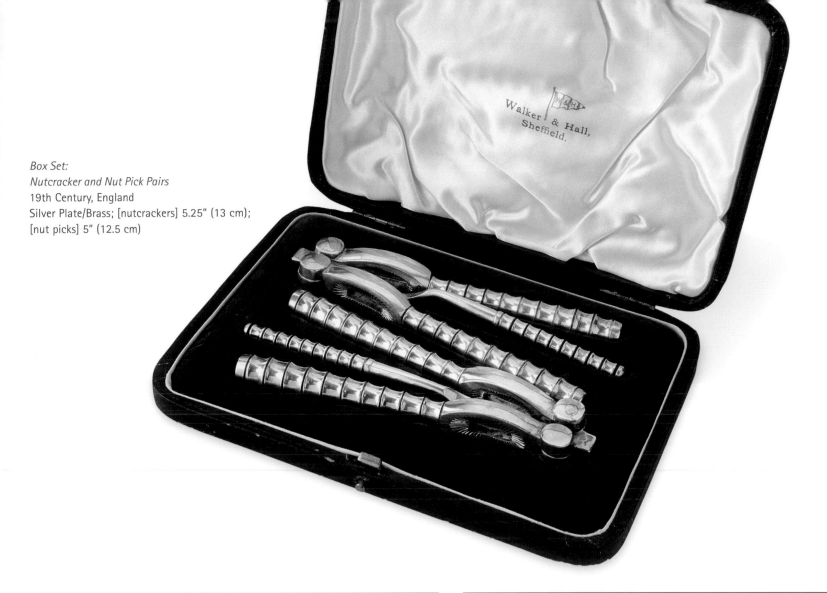

Box Set:
*Nutcracker and Nut Pick Pairs*
19th Century, England
Silver Plate/Brass; [nutcrackers] 5.25" (13 cm);
[nut picks] 5" (12.5 cm)

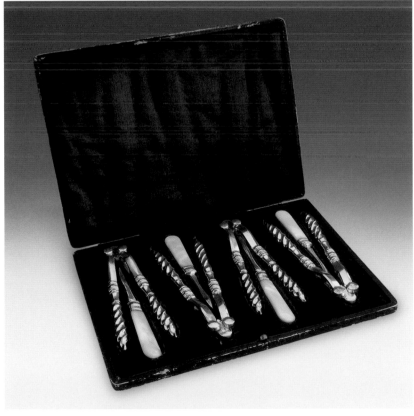

Box Set:
*Nutcrackers and Nut Picks with Mother-of-Pearl Handles*
19th Century, England
Silver Plate; [nutcrackers] 5.75" (14.5 cm); [nut picks] 5" (12.5 cm)

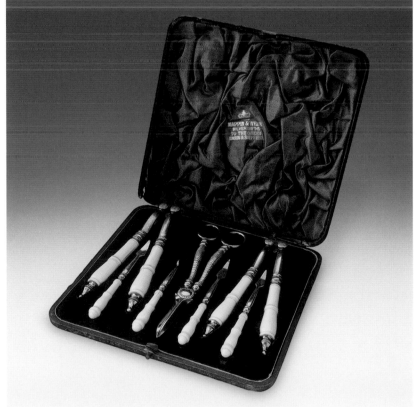

Box Set:
*Nutcrackers, Nut Picks, and Grape Shears*
19th Century, England
Silver Plate/Ivory Handles; [nutcrackers] 6" (15 cm); [nut picks] 4.5" (11.5 cm);
[shears] 6.75" (17 cm)

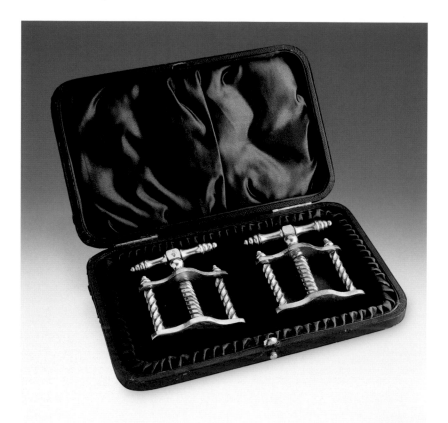

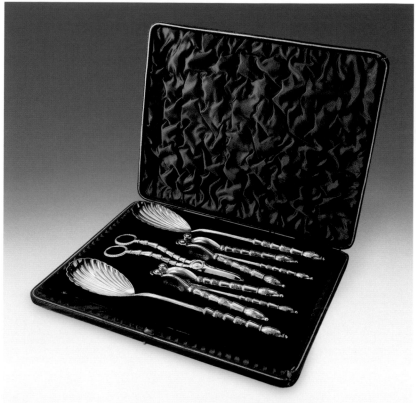

In 1878, a local dentist commissioned Henry M. Quackenbush to create steel dental tools. Recognizing that they could also be used as nutpicks, Quackenbush invented a nutcracker to sell with the nutpicks as a set.

*Box Set:*
*Quackenbush Nutcracker and Nut Picks*
19th Century, United States
Silver Plate/Brass; [nutcracker] 5" (12.5 cm);
[nut picks] 5.25" (13.5 cm)

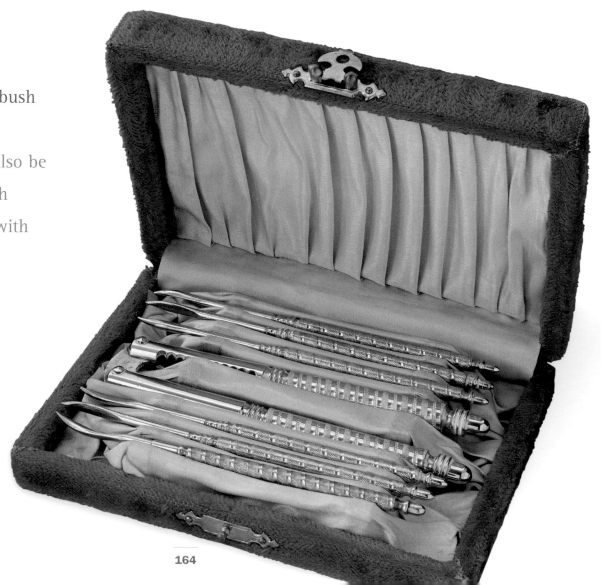

novel

# miscellaneous nutcrackers

Many of today's man-made materials are strong enough to withstand the rigors of cracking the hard shell of the nut. Nutcrackers crafted from these materials come in a variety of styles and colors, and are readily obtainable.

> *Nutcrackers may also reflect the humorous side of creativity.*

In some instances, nutcrackers were incorporated into other items—such as walking sticks or knives—which were carried by every well-dressed man during Victorian times. It was more common for a nutcracker head to simply be affixed to a walking stick, but one rare nutcracker-walking stick has been discovered that was carved from a single piece of wood. This piece of folk art shows snakes crawling up the staff, each devouring a frog, as well as two salamanders scurrying smartly away.

Nutcrackers may also reflect the humorous side of creativity. They may take the shape of a beetle, a donkey, a water pump, or a few nuts and bolts. Sometimes nutcrackers are made just for fun: too big to actually crack a nut, or so little they can hide in a nutshell.

*Variable Pressure Nutcrackers*
20th Century, Germany/United States
[ball] Plastic; 4" (10 cm); [cage] Aluminum; 7.25" (18.5 cm);
[bowl] Aluminum; 2.25" (5.5 cm)

*Wood Beetle with Iron Mechanism*
20th Century, France
Walnut/Iron; 8.25" (21 cm)

*Donkey (Made of Horse Shoes)*
20th Century, United States
Iron (Cast and Forged); 7" (18 cm)

*Synthetic Material Nutcrackers*
20th Century, Europe
Plastic; [from left to right] 4.25" (11 cm);
2.5" (6.5 cm); 11" (28 cm); 6" (15 cm);
4.5" (11.5 cm)

*Remarkable Pelican*
Patented 1966, United States
Chrome; 6.75" (17 cm)

*Humorous Woodpeckers*
[left] 1933 (by Otto Ulbricht); [right] 1997 (by Otto's son, Christian Ulbricht),
Germany
Linden; [tallest] 5.5" (14 cm)

*Nuts, Bolts, and Washers*
20th Century, Germany
Iron/Steel; 6" (15 cm)

*Miniature Nutcrackers in Shells*
Late 20th Century, Germany
Linden/Walnut Shells; 3" (7.5 cm)

*Carved Walnuts*
Early 20th Century, China
Walnut Shells; 1.5" (3.5 cm)

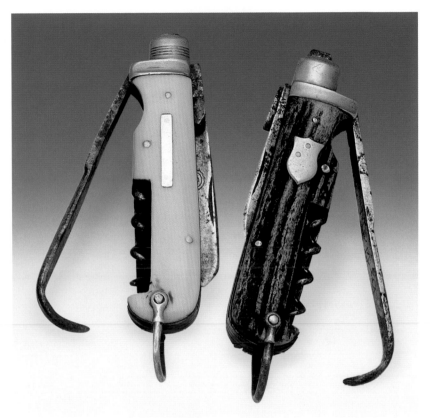

Pocket Knives with Nutcrackers
19th Century, England
Various Materials; 4.25" (11 cm)

Whimsical Lever Nutcracker
1950, Germany
Linden; 21.25" (54 cm)

Whimsical Lever Nutcracker (frontal view)
While attempting to crack a nut, this poor gnome
finds himself dangling in mid-air and must call for
assistance. "Help!"

*An Old-Fashioned Water Pump*
20th Century, United States
Aluminum; 8" (20.5 cm)

*One of the World's Smallest Nutcrackers*
2001, Germany
Poplar; 0.25" (5.1 mm)

*One of the World's Smallest Nutcrackers* (enlargement)
This tiny nutcracker was created specifically for The Leavenworth Nutcracker Museum by master carver of miniatures, Günter Werner Gotz of Germany.

*Nutcracker on a Matchstick* (full view)
This unique nutcracker, carved on the end of an ordinary matchstick, actually opens and closes its mouth when the back handle is operated.

*Nutcracker on a Matchstick*
1998, United States (Utah)
Poplar; 3" (7.5 cm)
*(This little fellow was carved for the Museum by John Bruce.)*

*Folk Art Walking Stick*
Late 18th/Early 19th Century, Central Europe
Conifer; 3.5' (1.07 m)

*Folk Art Walking Stick (detail)*
This nutcracker-walking stick is an amazing find, as it was carved from a single piece of wood. Snakes, frogs, and salamanders decorate the staff.

*Karl*
1980, Germany (Oberammergau)
Linden; 6.5' (1.98 m)
*(carved by Karl Rappl)*

*Cane Toppers*
19th Century, Switzerland
Walnut/Hazelnut/Silver; [full length] 37.5" (95.5 cm)

classic

# turned wooden toy soldier nutcrackers

*Soldier*
1880, Germany (Erzgebirge)
Spruce; 10.75" (27.5 cm)
*(crafted by Wilhelm Füchtner, "Father of the Nutcracker")*

The little village of Seiffen in the Erzgebirge (Ore Mountains) was founded in the 13th century as a mining town, as the wooded mountains contained silver, zinc, copper, iron, and other precious metals. Men worked hard in the mines most of the year, but in the long winter months they enjoyed working with wood and making simple toys or household articles.

> *As the popularity of the nutcracker grew, so did their designs.*

As ore began to deplete in the 17th century, the men turned more and more to their hobby of woodworking to earn a living for their families. The introduction of the lathe in the 16th century greatly aided the production of wooden articles. At first the lathes were foot-powered like an old-fashioned sewing machine, but by the middle of the 18th century, they were powered by the fast-running mountain streams. This coincided with the exhaustion of the ore, and production of wooden articles and toys greatly increased. The Erzgebirge region was soon famous for its handcrafted wooden products.

Although Seiffen is generally considered the birthplace of the wooden toy soldier, many authorities believe it first appeared in Sonneberg in the Thuringia region of Germany, which was already famous for its toy production. Records show that in 1735 there was mention of a "nut-biter" with a human look originating in Sonneberg. Men from this region went to the Erzgebirge to work in the mines, taking with them their toy-making skills. By 1745, nutcrackers from the Erzgebirge were being sold at the Dresden Fair and by street peddlers who carried their wares on their backs.

These nutcrackers were painted in bright colors with a water-based paint and shellacked. The basic body parts were turned on the lathe, but feet, mustache, and sometimes the eyes were created with a dough made of glue, wood flour, and water. Rabbit fur was generally used for the hair and beard. The nutcrackers were nearly always made as figures of authority such as kings, policemen, foresters, and military officers. The common people took great delight in having these figures of authority working for them in the lowly task of cracking nuts. Whereas the Sonneberg soldier had a cone-shaped hat, the Erzgebirge version took the shape of a miner's hat. As the popularity of the nutcracker grew, so did their designs, to include the familiar miner, fireman, chimney sweep, and town crier.

Since these nutcrackers were actually used in the homes to crack nuts and serve as toys for the children, they would soon show the damage of continued use. Most gave way to the fire for added warmth, and a new nutcracker was made for the family. It is difficult to find specimens of these early designs.

In 1872, Willhelm Füchtner (1844–1923) of Seiffen began the first commercial production of nutcrackers, making multiple figures from the same basic design turned on the lathe using spruce, beech, or alder. By changing hats, colors, and accessories, he made soldiers, kings, foresters, miners, and policemen. Known as the Father of the Nutcracker, Füchtner created designs that became the prototype for the Erzgebirge nutcrackers. These same basic designs are still being used today by the sixth generation of the Füchtner family.

Other makers who influenced the designs of early nutcrackers were Julius Glässer, Richard Langer, and Walter Tränkner.

It was at a Dresden street market that E. T. A. Hoffman saw his first nutcracker. This inspired him to write the story of "Nussknacker und Mausekönig" (Nutcracker and Mouse King), which was published in 1816. This book was the basis for the ballet composed by Peter Ilyich Tchaikovsky and choreographed by Marius Petipa. It was first performed in Russia in 1892, and introduced in the United States by the San Francisco Ballet in 1944.

Today over 200 ballet companies, both large and small, annually produce *The Nutcracker* in the United States. More than 2 million people see live productions on stage each year, and millions more see it on television or on the movie screen. The popularity of *The Nutcracker* has made the wooden toy soldier nutcracker a very desirable gift or collectible. Tens of thousands of these lovable, toothy characters are sold each year. People are captivated by their charm, and their presence brings a festive note to the holiday season.

The demand for the nutcracker also was increased greatly by United States soldiers stationed in Germany after World War II. Intrigued by the nutcrackers they found at street fairs and markets, they sent many home to family and friends.

By this time, the Erzgebirge was separated from the main part of Germany, and the factories were owned by the new communist government, which controlled the designs and distribution. As the popularity of the nutcracker grew, special designs were made for the American market, such as the cowboy, pilot, and fisherman. Almost all of the production was sent to the United States in return for the American dollar. While the Erzgebirge makers still used the traditional body style, several makers who escaped to the western zones began producing more creative designs. Christian Steinbach settled in the town of Hohenhameln, the Otto Ulbricht family in Lauingen, Günter Ulbricht in Muggendorf, and Volkmar Matthes near Stuttgart.

The second half of the 20th century brought hundreds of new nutcracker designs to meet the passion of collectors, thousands of whom are in the United States. After the reunification of Germany, the Erzgebirge companies again were privatized, and new designs flourished. Today the collector can find storybook characters, sports figures, professionals, Santas, and even American Indian chiefs. Although many new shapes and styles have emerged, the classic wooden toy soldier of the Erzgebirge remains the outstanding favorite.

*Sonneberg King*
1880, Germany (Thuringia)
Turned and Carved Wood; 9" (23 cm)

*Miners*
[right] 1880 (by Wilhelm Füchtner); [left] 1998 (by Familie Füchtner)
Germany (Erzgebirge)
Spruce; [tallest] 14.5" (36.5 cm)

*Familie Füchtner King*
1920, Germany (Erzgebirge)
Spruce; 13.5" (34.5 cm)

*Miners (detail)*
The symbol featured on these nutcrackers is that of an
Erzgebirge miner. Many of the miners had dress uniforms
for special occasions. Descendants of these early laborers
still don similar uniforms for parades and festivals.

The Brothers Grimm began their dictionary of High German in 1830, and the word *Nussknacker* appeared. It was described as "often in the form of a miniature little man, in whose mouth the nut, by means of lever or screw, is cracked open."

*Two Sonneberg Soldiers*
Early 20th Century, Germany (Thuringia)
Various Woods; 18" (45 cm)
*(Conical-shaped hats are typical of Sonneberg nutcrackers.)*

*Napoleon*
1820, Germany (Thuringia)
Various Woods/Paper Maché; 11.5" (29 cm)

*Soldier*
1880, Germany (Erzgebirge)
Spruce; 10.75" (27.5 cm)
*(crafted by Wilhelm Füchtner, "Father of the Nutcracker")*

*Early Erzgebirge Nutcrackers*
Middle 20th Century, Germany (Erzgebirge)
Various Woods; [from left to right] 16" (40.5 cm); 15.5" (39.5 cm); 11.5" (29 cm); 14" (35.5 cm)
*(crafted by Julius Glässer, Walter Tränkner, and Richard Langer)*

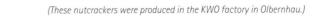
*Erzgebirge Solders*
Late 20th/Early 21st Century, Germany
Beech/Alder; [tallest] 12" (30.5 cm)
*(These nutcrackers were produced in the KWO factory in Olbernhau.)*

*Conductor, Blue King, Red King, and Soldier*
1978, Germany (Lauingen)
Linden/Beech; [tallest] 13.75" (35 cm); [smallest] 9.75" (24.5 cm)
*(These were the first nutcrackers produced in the Holzkunst Christian Ulbricht factory in 1978.)*

*Military Officers*
Late 20th Century, Germany
Pine/Beech/Ash/Birch; [tallest] 18" (45.5 cm)
*(by Volkmar Matthes)*

*Soldier, Prince, and King*
Late 20th Century, Germany (Erzgebirge)
Linden/Beech/Alder; [from left to right] 11.75" (30 cm);
15.5" (39.5 cm); 9" (23 cm)
*(from the Seiffener Nussknackerhaus)*

*Wizard of Oz Characters*
Late 20th Century, Germany
Linden/Beech/Birch/Mahogany; [from left to right] 20" (51 cm);
16" (40.5 cm); 15.25" (38.5 cm); 20" (51 cm)
*(by Christian Ulbricht)*

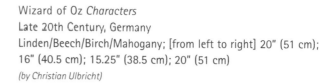

*Folk Art Nutcrackers*
Late 20th Century, Austria
[from left to right] 10.5" (26.5 cm);
Beech/Birch; 10.5" (26.5 cm); 14" (35.5 cm)

*Musketeer, Chimney Sweep, Fireman, and King*
1970, Germany (Erzgebirge)
Molded Sawdust/Glue Mixture and Wood; [largest] 15.75" (40 cm)
*(These nutcrackers with the "Vero" label were made in the German Democratic Republic.)*

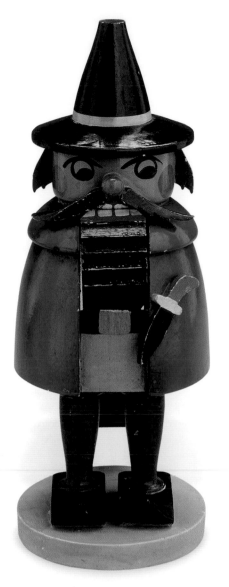

*Thief (by Wendt & Kühn)*
1938, Germany (Erzgebirge)
Beech; 10.25" (26 cm)

*Musketeer, Sportsman, Rose Cavalier (by Rauscher)*
Late 20th/Early 21st Century, Germany (Nürnberg)
Linden/Lime Wood; [largest] 14.75" (37.5 cm)

*Hunter, Mountain Man, Viking*
Late 20th Century, Germany (Erzgebirge)
Beech/Alder/Ash; [largest] 16.25" (41.5 cm)
(by E. K. Müller)

*Soldier, Scotsman, Captain*
Late 20th Century, Germany
Linden; [largest] 13.75" (35 cm)
(These figures were turned by Hanno Junghänel, son of Lothar Junghänel.)

*King and Town Crier*
1947, Germany
Linden/Maple/Beech; [left] 11.75" (30 cm);
[right] 13.5" (34.5 cm)
*(These are Christian Steinbach's first nutcrackers.)*

*Chimney Sweep and Night Watchman*
1980, Germany
Pine; 11" (28 cm)
*(These nutcrackers were made by Otto Ulbricht, father of Christian Ulbricht.)*

*Soldiers (from the Dieter Legler Factory)*
Late 20th Century, Germany (Erzgebirge)
Beech; [from left to right] 16" (40.5 cm); 9" (23 cm);
11.5" (29 cm); 14" (35.5 cm)

*Festive Nutcrackers (Petersen Design)*
Germany; Birch
[from left to right] 1970, 10.5" (26.5 cm);
1980, 15.5" (39.5 cm); 1980, 23.5" (60.5 cm);
1960, 12" (30.5 cm)

*Drinking Buddies*
Late 20th Century, Germany (Erzgebirge)
Spruce/Birch/Beech; [large] 13.25" (33.5 cm);
[small] 7" (18 cm)
*(by Richard Glässer of Seiffen)*

*Drinking Buddies (detail)*
The HB ligature seen on many nutcrackers stands for
the Hofbraühaus, a venerable beer hall in Munich well
known for its annual Oktoberfest celebration.

*Camelot Collection (by Steinbach)*
1991, Germany
Beech; [largest] 19.75" (50 cm)

183

*Assembled Nutcracker/Individual Components*
Late 20th Century, Germany (Erzgebirge)
Beech; 12.75" (32.5 cm)
(by Olaf Kolbe)

*Nutcracker Suite*
Late 20th Century, Germany
Linden/Beech/Birch; [tallest] 16" (40.5 cm); [shortest] 11.5" (29 cm)
(by Christian Ulbricht)

It takes approximately 130 procedures to make a turned wooden toy soldier nutcracker, from the initial cutting of the wood to the final packaging. Some of these nutcrackers are made in small family workshops, while others are produced in large factories that employ many skilled craftsmen.

185

*Closing:*
# The Leavenworth Nutcracker Museum Today

The Leavenworth Nutcracker Museum, a National Heritage Foundation, is a nonprofit 501(c)(3), 509(a)(1) foundation dedicated to fostering and encouraging interest of the general public in the history of nutcrackers, their creators, and the importance of nuts in the diets of peoples throughout history.

The museum is located in Leavenworth, Washington, a small Bavarian village nestled in the eastern foothills of the Cascade Range. Leavenworth captured the title of the A&E Network's "Ultimate Holiday Town USA" for 2003. With its Bavarian architecture, clear, clean rivers, and a backdrop of steep mountains, our village attracts over 1.3 million tourists a year. It is truly the perfect place for The Leavenworth Nutcracker Museum.

The museum opened its doors to the public in June 1995, occupying approximately 1,500 square feet on the second floor of the Nussknacker Haus building. In December 2001, The Leavenworth Nutcracker Museum was accepted as part of the National Heritage Foundation. The entire collection of nutcrackers and the building have been donated to the National Heritage Foundation to ensure that the collection will stay together for many generations to enjoy.

In May 2002, the museum was enlarged to encompass the whole second floor of 3,000 square feet. Nutcrackers that had been in storage for years finally found their place in the many newly added cases. The *History of Nutcrackers* video presentation for visitors was upgraded, and a lift was installed to accommodate persons with disabilities.

Since the opening of the museum, there have been visitors from forty-one different countries, seven of the nine Canadian provinces, and forty-nine of the fifty United States. While most visitors are familiar with the wooden toy soldier so often seen at Christmastime and the metal handheld nutcracker in their kitchens, nearly everyone is amazed to see such a variety. As one guest put it, *"This is nutcracker heaven!"*

The museum's website, www.nutcrackermuseum.com, provides much information on nutcrackers, as well as history and the nutritional value of nuts. Additionally, a website designed for student use can be found at www.kidslovenutcrackers.com. A book is being written for children to give them an introduction to nutcrackers, including the many kinds of nutcrackers, how they work, how the wooden toy soldiers are made, and the unusual ways a nut can be cracked.

Over the years we have seen many different nutcracker collections. Some collectors prefer only wooden toy soldiers, others the metal or wood carved figural designs, the mechanical, or the betel cutters. Others will, as we did, choose a variety. But no matter what kind of nutcrackers you collect, my husband and I offer one little piece of advice: Remember, once you start collecting, it's almost impossible to stop! Proof is in The Leavenworth Nutcracker Museum.

—Arlene Wagner, *The Nutcracker Lady*

*Karl*
1980, Germany (Oberammergau)
6.5' (1.98 m)
*(carved by Karl Rappl)*

enduring

# Acknowledgments

JUDITH RITTENHOUSE

*Ornamental and Figural Nutcrackers*, Collector Books, 1993

ROBERT MILLS

*Nutcrackers*, Shire Books, 2001

JONATHAN LEVI

*Treen for the Table*, Antique Collectors Club, 1998

EDWARD H. PINTO

*Treen and Other Wooden Bygones*, Bell & Hyman, 1969

HENRY RENÉ D'ALLEMAGNE

*Decorative Antique Ironwork*, Dover Publications, 1968

PHILLY RAINS AND DONALD BULL

*Anri Woodcarvings*, Schiffer Publishing Co., 2001

JAMES ROLLBAND

*American Nutcrackers*, Off Beat Books, 1996

HENRY BROWNRIGG

*Betel Cutters*, Thomas & Hudson Ltd., 1992

PAOLO DE SANCTIS E MAURIZIO FANTONI

*Schiaccianoci*, Autorizzazione del Tribunale di Milano, 1987

HELLMUT BILZ

*Erzgebirgische Volkskunst*, Ingo Beer Verlag, 1997

ADOLF HEIDENREICH

*Nutcrackers, Shape and History*, Käthe Wohlfahrt GmbH & Co. OHG, 2003

*Pocket Screw*
18th Century, England
Bone; 3.25" (8 cm)